What Othe... ....

Katrina's messages are consistently inspiring and are a call to action. Is she a bug on my wall? How does she know what message to share at just the right time in my life?

—**Cindy Nixon-Witt,**
Coach-Consultant, personal & professional development

I can't begin to say how much these messages have impacted my life. I have always seemed to read them at just the right time, and they appeared to be written just for me. Actually, I'm positive they were written just for me because even before God formed me, He had already seen my days and already supplied the need. These messages have become a vital part of my spiritual nourishment. They have been and I'm sure will continue to be a tremendous blessing. Thank you, Katrina, for being a willing and obedient vessel that He is using to transform lives...

—**Janice Eichelberger,**
Program Coordinator, Department of Health
and Environmental Control

Katrina's messages are on it. So close, they touched me. Katrina is being used in ways that directly let me know God is in the "current" and she is the wire. I am thankful she is reaching out and making the "connection." The souls of people are crying out for messages like these.

—**Charlene "Chiccy Baritone" Evans,**
Poet and Author, *"Next In Line"*

Katrina has done it again. It is so amazing how I get confirmation after confirmation on the issues in my life. The messages are truly inspirational and a blessing to me. I thank God for allowing her to reach me and others with her words.

—**Tyece Roundtree,**
College Student

The messages in this book are powerful and always timely reminders. I am thankful that Katrina is using her blessed giftedness to assist others on the journey. I especially thank her for blessing my life.

—Kathy Csank,
Senior Liaison, Collaboration for Ministry Initiative

Katrina, it is so wonderful to be used by God as a vessel fit for the Master's use. My prayer is that you continue to saturate yourself with the Word of God so that these wonderful illustrations, devotions, and inspirations can be manifested to you to share with the entire world.

—Helena Cain,
Youth Minister

As the Co-founder and editor of a Christian magazine, I look for material that addresses the heart of man and the heart of Jesus. Katrina Spigner's devotionals often reflect both. I love her transparency. I believe deep down we all long for our masks to be removed. Her epiphany becomes my epiphany as I consider how closely her words mirror the heart of Scripture.

—Anne Buck,
Reach Out Columbia

The thoughts of inspiration Katrina provides are relevant and timeless . The principles she offers are universal and beneficial to anyone who would choose to apply them. Her personal experiences illustrate to every reader that we all face the same challenges, and yet, there are ways to overcome.

—Betty M. Parker,
Author,
Waging War On Fear: Strategies to Overcome a Scary World

This is for
YOU!

This is for YOU!

31 Days of Life Changing Discoveries

Katrina Spigner

Pleasant Word
A Division of WINEPRESS PUBLISHING

Pleasant Word (a division of WinePress Publishing, PO Box 428, Enumclaw, WA 98022) functions only as book publisher. As such, the ultimate design, content, editorial accuracy, and views expressed or implied in this work are those of the author.

Unless otherwise noted, all Scriptures are taken from the *Holy Bible, New King James Version*, copyright 1979, 1980, 1982, Thomas Nelson, Inc. Publishers.

ISBN 13: 978-1-4141-1224-4
ISBN 10: 1-4141-1224-6
Library of Congress Catalog Card Number: 2008903344

To my heavenly Father, the author and finisher of my faith. And to the memory of my earthly father, Minister Tryon Eichelberger, Jr., who always believed that God had great things in store for my life and who modeled faith, integrity, and patience, leaving me with the foundational legacy upon which I stand.

Contents

⎯⁓⁑○

Part III: My Emotions

Preface

THIS BOOK TAKES a unique and stimulating approach to challenging and inspiring people of all ages and of diverse backgrounds. The book differs from any other personal growth or inspirational book in that the focus of each chapter is on the investigation, uncovering, and integration of God's plans and purpose for your spiritual and personal life.

Every day, for 31 days, the book challenges you to investigate where you are on your spiritual journey, while seeking where God planned for you to be. As a result of your personal explorations, you will uncover hidden treasures that have been buried deep within the fertile ground of your soul (your will, your mind, and your emotions). Ultimately, your inquisitive excavations will unearth nuggets of gold that can be integrated into every aspect of your journey toward living on purpose.

In each daily reading you will find reality-based experiences as well as insightful and thought-provoking opportunities to delve into the discovery of God's personalized intentions for your life. This will be done in three distinctive sections:

"This Is for You" will stimulate your thinking while inspiring and challenging you to pursue all God has ordained for your life.

"God's Word to You" will guide you into Scripture passages where God can reveal His truth through His Word.

"Journal Discovery" will challenge you to deeply reflect on your life while approaching each question honestly and thoughtfully. In the process, you will understand and apply your own personal lessons, goals, and strategies.

Acknowledgments

THIS BOOK IS the result of the prayers, support, and encouragement of many people.

First of all, my loving thanks to Jamil and Kayla—the mention of your names brings joy to my heart. I am blessed among women to have the two of you as my children. We have faced some challenging times together. But, we have seen the hand of God move mightily in our lives. Thank you for your unwavering love and respect. You have consistently provided strength, motivation, and lessons for my journey. As John S. Mbiti, the noted philosopher, once wrote, "I am because we are; and because we are, I am." I love you my babies.

I must thank my sister Kristie. On many occasions you have openly stated your love and admiration for me—now, it's my turn. You have been my support system through this entire project. You tirelessly read copy after copy after copy without complaining. You listened to my ideas and concepts and always offered feedback with enthusiasm and excitement. Although my name is on the cover of this book, your spirit is hidden within the content of each page. I love you and am eternally grateful to have you in my life.

To my sister Kimberly, my cheerleader, biggest fan, and undercover publicist—thank you for forwarding my writing all over North Carolina. With every accomplishment in my life, your words, "Well, alright," have meant more than I can express. I am eagerly anticipating the fulfillment of your prophetic vision for G.I.F.T. I love you.

Well, Mamma Ollie, what do you think? I have asked you that question all my life, and today your answer still matters. Thank you for your maternal love. You have not only held me in your heart, but also you have held me in high esteem. Thank you for always supporting me, for having my back, and for being my truest friend.

Thank you to my pastor, Dr. Derrick W. Hutchins, for helping me understand that I had gifts inside of me when I did not know it and could not see it. Thank you for making me go get the towel every time I threw it in and for insisting that I pursue all God has purposed and planned for me. Your role in my life has been undeniably life-changing.

Bernadette, I am so excited about the release of our co-authored book, *Joined at the Heart: The Real Meaning of Friendship.* I thank God for every lesson He has taught us and for our precious journey together. Thank you for your insight, support, assistance, and ideas for this project. But most of all, thank you for your unconditional love.

Jo, I am so thankful for your friendship, tears, encouragement, prayers, and most of all, your laughter. Thank you for your heartfelt responses to my writing and for your never-ending support. I am so humbled by the fact that you began making plans for this book long before its completion. I truly appreciate that God placed you in my life—my "real" friend.

Bernetta and Camille, thank you for the "girl-talk" and for providing me with meaningful relationships with both of you where I can just be me. Camille, because you were a forerunner in this process, you readily shared useful information. Thank you for giving unselfishly. Bernetta, thank you for your feedback and for the significance you placed on these messages. The fact that you find value in each lesson means more than you know. I really do want to be like both of you when I grow up.

Anna, as promised. Thank you for believing in me and for helping me find my voice. I assure you it will never be silenced again.

Cindy, thank you for helping me find the missing pieces to my purpose puzzle. You have been an encouragement and inspiration through this entire process and beyond, and I am so very grateful. I know that the best for us is yet to come.

To my weekly G.I.F.T. subscribers—I truly appreciate your subscription and the encouraging responses you send. Many of you were a catalyst for putting these messages into book form, and for that I am eternally grateful.

To the women I have coached along the way—thank you for inviting me to be a part of your lives and for allowing me to point you toward purpose. I am amazed and blessed by the gifts of God that are innate within each of you. I am confident of this very thing, "That He who has begun a good work in you will complete it until the day of Jesus Christ" (Philippians 1:6).

Last, but not least, thank you to all who will use this book to make life-changing discoveries toward living a purposeful life. This really is for you.

Oh, and thank you so much to my footstools (Psalm 110:1). You have been an invaluable part of my journey. God bless you.

Introduction

~∭©

ON THE THIRD day of my first week of second grade, my mother scurried through the house in an effort to get me ready for school. We were both still trying to get used to the idea of my being dropped off at my grandma's house to catch the school bus. This was a different schedule than the one to which we had grown accustomed. Although we lived in a small, rural town, prior to this time I had been able to ride into the city with my mother to go to school. On her way, she would drop me off at the door of my first grade class.

My elementary school was a quality, historically black school that was strategically placed in the middle of the inner city. It was a testament to the community and was just blocks away from my mother's office at one of the top historically black colleges in South Carolina.

As we walked to the car, my mother asked me a second time, "Are you sure you have everything you need?"

I said, "Yes, Ma'am," and we were on our way.

She pulled into the driveway at Grandma's house, helped me with the car door, kissed me goodbye, and began her commute.

Grandma greeted me at the door with a big smile and her usual, "Hurry in here so you can eat before that bus gets here." Grandma was also responsible for putting two of my cousins on the bus. So we all sat and ate together with Grandma hurrying us along every thirty seconds. We giggled at her threats of not taking us to school if we missed the bus.

As we finished our breakfast, grabbed our books, and headed for the door, it hit me—I didn't have anything for the first day of show and tell. Immediately, I reflected on my mom's deliberate reminder earlier and began to cry. It was my intent to hide my tears from Grandma, but absolutely nothing ever got past her.

She quickly asked, "Child, what's wrong with you?"

I explained to her that I had left my item for show and tell at home.

"Is that all?" She quickly looked around the room with her hands perched on her hips. Because all of the community kids played here, and because she threw absolutely nothing away that came into her possession, I'm sure she believed she could find me something in a hurry. She walked over to the corner where my male cousins had been playing and picked up an item and put it in my hand. "Here, take this to show and tell—now come on so you can catch that bus."

When I looked in my hand I saw that Grandma had handed me the largest marble I had ever seen. It was utterly beautiful. It was blue, black, and grey. Although I didn't exactly know what I was going to tell about it, I knew that I couldn't wait for everybody in my class to see it.

As the bus pulled up to the breezeway in the back of the school, I got the same nervous, sinking feeling that I had felt two days before. Things just weren't the same since my parents had been required to enroll me in this elementary school. It was zoned for integration. This school had been occupied by whites only. However, almost a year after Dr. Martin Luther King Jr.'s death, here we were.

I walked into my class, put my marble and books in the cubby portion of my desk, and took my seat. We began the day with the Lord's Prayer, the Pledge of Allegiance, and the singing of "My Country Tis of Thee."

My teacher was a tall, older Caucasian woman with shiny silver hair. She probably would have appeared more attractive to me had it not been for the seemingly constant scowl on her face. She did not try to hide her disdain toward those of us who were new to the school. Nevertheless, I believed that this day would be different. I would be able to stand in front of the class and talk, show my marble, win my teacher's affection, and make new friends in the process.

At the end of the scholastic portion of the day, finally it was time for show and tell. The teacher announced that we could take out our items and wait our turn to be called upon. She began to give us directives regarding the order we would come to the front. However, as she was completing her instructions, the white boy sitting next to me reached over into my desk's cubby and took my marble. After a few seconds of disbelief, I emphatically stated, "That is my marble. You can't have my marble." While staking my claim, I raised my hand to get the teacher's attention.

After a moment, she acknowledged my hand by asking, "What is it?" I told her that my classmate had just taken my marble out of my desk. She walked over to where we were both sitting and asked him if he had taken my marble. His words to her were an emphatic, "No, I did not take that nigger's marble."

She turned to me and sternly uttered, "Don't you ever lie to me again." She turned and walked away.

I watched silently as this little boy told a story and showed the class my marble. I was absolutely devastated. In my six years on earth, I had never felt that kind of pain. In a matter of moments, my entire world had been reframed. I had been robbed of my innocence, security, and stability and left with guilt, fear, and uncertainty. The heated rod of injustice had branded the core of my soul—into my will, my mind, and my emotions. As a result, I suffered the greatest loss of all…my voice.

Consequently, my inability to speak out set in motion a traumatic, arduous journey filled with a lack of power, confidence, purpose, independence, and peace. It veiled my eyes, ears, heart, and mind concerning the good plans that had been ordained for my life. I spent a significant amount of time in search of reassurance. I searched for self-assurance. I searched for direction. I searched for autonomy. I searched for authenticity. I searched for permanence. I searched and searched for the same beauty and awe in life that I saw in my marble that day in 1969. I searched with a drive and determination to get my marble back. As a result, I began my own personal journey of life-changing discoveries with God.

Although your losses may not be the same as the ones I have encountered, at some point in your life you have experienced the trauma of having various components of yourself taken away that were vital to your living your life on purpose.

As we journey together for the next 31 days, it is my sincere hope and prayer that you will make discoveries that will change your life and that you will recover your own marbles while making a commitment never to lose them again.

Let Us Pray

Father, as I embark upon this journey of discovery, I ask that you guide me into all truths. I believe that over the next 31 days you will make plain to me who I really am and who you have created me to be. As I proceed, help me to search for and uncover those things that have hindered me from fulfilling my purpose. As I examine my soul and surrender what I find to you, I trust you to help me make the changes and adjustments that are needed. Help me recover all of your blessings that, over the course of my life, I have lost—blessings that are necessary components for fulfilling the plans you have for my life. I commit myself and this process to you. I thank you for renewing my will, my mind, and my emotions. I give you the honor and glory for doing a new thing in me.

In the name of Jesus,

Amen.

Today's Date_____10/25/09_____

Let the journey begin …

Part I

My Will

Are You up for the Challenge?

Our real problem, then, is not our strength today; it is rather the vital necessity of action today to ensure our strength tomorrow.

—Dwight D. Eisenhower

FOR A VERY long time I had said to myself that I needed to get in shape. Prior to turning forty-something, I had done wonderfully well with managing my weight. I could eat whatever I wanted without being concerned about an impact on my "girlish" figure. However, it seems the day I turned forty, my metabolism decided to enter into retirement.

I believe it literally gave up trying to burn off excess calories from all the foods I loved and left me to fend for myself. In fact, the evidence of my metabolic dysfunction was very apparent every time I looked at my disrobed body in the mirror. It was as if I could hear the lyrics of a popular oldie playing in the back of my mind regarding saying goodbye to yesterday. For the first time in my life I began to see the cruelty in the laws of gravity, and I felt defenseless against its pull.

Nevertheless, after a season of woe and dismay, I made a decision for a lifestyle change and hired a personal trainer. After speaking to my trainer on the phone, I was invited to come to the fitness center for an orientation. When I arrived, he discussed the sessions and informed me that our focus would primarily be on strength and resistance training.

He talked about the beginning process and then took me on a tour of the facility. As I began my walk through the building, the first thing I noticed was an environment saturated with bright lights, mirrors, and other trainers with trainees. I watched as each trainer offered the trainees motivational phrases such as, "You can do it!" and "You're almost there!" I watched as all the trainees met the goal their personal trainer had set before them, no matter how heavy the weight, no matter how much stress was being placed on the muscle, and no matter how hard they had to inhale, exhale, or yell. What's more interesting is, while the trainer was the one who had developed the strict regimen of exercise and demanded that every exercise repetition be carried out, at the end of the grueling sessions, the trainees celebrated and praised the trainer for taking them through a good workout.

They gave hugs and high-fives in a way that demonstrated great appreciation for the pain and struggle they had just endured. Why? Because they wanted the same thing I was looking for—results. After what I had seen, I left my orientation asking myself one simple question, "Are you up for the challenge?" I answered that question with an emphatic "Yes!"

I returned to the center two days later for my first workout with my trainer. I began the first half of my session with a warm-up. The stretches were not bad, the treadmill was not too hard, and the beginner weights were not that heavy. However, as we moved into the second half of the session, the trainer decided to pick up the pace. He programmed the treadmill to elevate and double the speed. When I got off the treadmill, while I was still searching for my next breath, he had me screaming through exercises with weights that felt as though I was lifting small cars. And, much to my dismay, all of this was happening under those bright lights, with me seeing my distorted face in those mirrors, and with seemingly everybody watching. At that point, with every labored breath, with every heavier weight, with more eyes on me than comfortable, my "yes" began to turn into a "maybe," and then into an "I don't know," and then into an "I don't think so." Finally it settled into an "I must have lost my mind."

But, on my way to a "no," the trainer stepped beside me and got down by my ear with these phrases: "Come on, Katrina, you can do it." "You are almost there." "One last push."

And so it is with our lives. We are often faced with various challenges—some we take on ourselves, and some are placed in our paths by others. When we are called to meet the challenge, what we are really being asked is, "Are you ready to put forth the extraordinary effort that will be required of you to get the results you desire?"

Often times we are quick to say "yes" without understanding that God's primary focus for this challenge will be strength and resistance training. So, in the midst of the challenge, when the lights are on us, and the pressure is being applied and the weight is increasing and everybody is watching and we are seeing a view of ourselves we have never seen before...what happens to our "yes"?

This Is for You: As you are called to challenges, look to God—your Personal Trainer. Calm down long enough to hear Him saying in your ear, "You can do all things." Remember, He is the one who developed your training regimen anyway. His goal for you is filled with plans to strengthen you and to build your resistance. He knows the results you desire and the results desired for you. Don't allow the pain and weights to cause you to change your "yes" to "no" in the face of your challenges. Stay up for the challenge. And, when you finally make it to the end of your training session, celebrate and praise your Personal Trainer for how He "works-out" your life.

God's Word to You: "I can do all things through Christ who strengthens me" (Philippians 4:13).

Day One Journal Discovery

1. Life's challenges are often used to build strength and resistance.
    What are your most pressing challenges at this time in your life?
    Have you turned away from them? If so, why?

    Accepting things that I can not change, realizing that I am me and I have the power to do some things for myself. Having peace in my life! Hearing what you say God.

2. What changes are you willing to make in order to say "yes" to
    the specific challenges set before you?

    Listen harder for God to speak and live his "Will" for me not mine.

3. How will saying "yes" move you closer to living on purpose?

    Welcoming God everyday into my life and thanking him more for showing favor on me. Loving my God & following his will for my life.

Private Lessons

*There is no royal road to learning; no short cut to the acquirement
of any valuable lesson.*

—Anthony Trollope

ON A SUNDAY morning, several years ago, I walked into the sanctuary
at my local church during the praise and worship portion of our service.
As I made my way to the balcony, I noticed the worshipers all around
me up on their feet leaping, shouting in acclamation, and clapping their
hands in seemingly sincere celebration. But, as others stood around me
in exuberant corporate participation, I took my seat. Consumed with the
frustration I had brought to church with me that day, I sat and observed
while pondering the questions that ran rapidly through my mind. *God,
why am I here? What is all the hoopla about? How long is all this going to
take? How much of this is really necessary anyway?*

As my eyes filled with tears, I could not understand why during a time
when I should have felt the most enthused, energetic, and demonstrative
about my spiritual walk, I sat lethargically, discouraged, with a deep
sense of dissatisfaction, and hopelessly questioning my salvation and
my purpose. I had been a Christian for years. I had worked and held
leadership positions in ministry. And, up until this point in my life, I
really believed that I had a strong relationship with the Lord. However,

now I felt more agitated, aggravated, and discombobulated than I had ever felt in my entire life, and I was wondering how I had gotten to this place. To make matters worse, I felt as though I was invisible, like nobody else could really see me. I also felt as if I was the only one who was going through (or who had ever gone through) this experience.

Here I sat, a single mother of two, working two part-time jobs, going to school to earn my bachelor's degree in the evenings, and now back at home living with my mother.

My marriage had failed, and my father had gone on to be with the Lord. I had been scrutinized and judged by others. And at this point, my whole soul had been shaken by the grief associated with the many, many losses I had encountered in my life. It seemed that everything in me hurt. Inhaling and exhaling no longer felt like a normal body function for me. Instead it had become an agonizing, laborious act of survival.

I never imagined that life could wound me to the extent that I could literally take it or leave it. But the vicissitudes of living had beaten up on my will to the degree that there seemed to be no recovery from the trauma. I felt as though Jesus Himself had given Satan permission to sift me as wheat, but I was not sure if anyone was praying that my faith would not fail me. Therefore, in the midst of this huge congregation of people, I felt more alone than I had ever felt before, and I was angry. As a matter of fact, at that very moment, I felt as though I could have stood up in the middle of the service, walked down to the front of the sanctuary, asked the worship leader to hand me the microphone, and screamed at the top of my lungs, "Shut up! Everybody just shut up and sit down right now."

But instead, in that service, in the midst of my personal despair, in a last act of desperation, I asked God to help me. And, during my deepest lamentation, I heard this message in my spirit. "Now that I finally have your attention, let me teach you something." At that very moment, I realized God had orchestrated that place of emptiness and despondency because He had something He wanted me to learn. My private, inner turmoil was directly related to the private lessons He desired to teach me.

This Is for You: Consider the definition of a "private lesson." It is "A course of instruction that is unique to the student that he or she can only learn through study or experience, and takes place separate from the company or observation of others." A description of a private lesson for a student of dance stated, "Taking dance lessons is a good way to learn choreography of a form, but individualized instruction is necessary if a student wishes to advance to higher levels. A private session with a perceptive teacher is one of the best ways to accelerate your personal progress."

And so it is with God. When He knows our sincere desire to go to the next level, He does not leave us as we are. As our perceptive teacher, He moves us out of the status quo, and He leads us into wilderness experiences that are unique to us, so He can teach us lessons that will accelerate our personal progress. Why? The reasons are simple. He wants us to demonstrate what He has accomplished in us as a result of His individualized instruction in our lives. He wants our lives to manifest the excellence that is only obtained through one-on-one sessions. In other words, it is extremely important to Him that we learn private lessons so that He can trust us in our public performance. Our response should simply be, "Where do I sign up?"

God's Word to You: "And you shall remember that the Lord your God led you all the way these forty years in the wilderness, to humble you and test you, to know what was in your heart, whether you would keep His commandments or not" (Deuteronomy 8:2).

Day Two Journal Discovery

1. In what way(s) do you believe God has tried to get your attention so He can teach you something?

    With my children + my husband. When things are not right with them it affects me and I call on Jesus more because that seems to be when I am most at "peace".

2. How has your "public performance" been affected because of your avoidance of your personal private lessons? What adjustments do you need to make in an effort to use your lessons to the purpose for which they were given to you?

    Half done, not complete

3. How will you use the lessons in your life to move you closer to living on purpose?

    Sitting still and listening for God's lessons, accept them as opportunities instead of failures.

Enough

*Since wars begin in the minds of men, it is in the minds of men
that the defenses of peace must be constructed.*

—Author unknown

ONE OF MY favorite movies of all times is *Enough,* starring Jennifer
Lopez. I have watched this motion picture a number of times, and I
am left with a greater appreciation of the main character's journey after
each viewing. In the storyline, Slim is working as a waitress when she
marries Mitch. Basking in self-perceived marital ecstasy, Slim believes
she is entering a life of domestic bliss with the man of her dreams. After
the arrival of their first child, her picture-perfect life is shattered when
she discovers Mitch's hidden, possessive dark side. He turns out to be
a controlling and abusive man and fills her life with terror. Frightened
for her child's safety, Slim flees with her daughter. However, relentless
in his pursuit, Mitch continually stalks them. Finally, Slim is forced to
fight back. She engages Mitch in a physical and psychological battle,
showing him that she's had *enough.*

According to *The American Heritage Dictionary*, the word "enough"
is used to express impatience or exasperation. While I am completely
aware that the cinematography of the movie did a superb job engaging
the viewer mentally, emotionally, and even physically, the dramatizations

capture a real-life message that many of us face or have faced on our own journeys.

In fact, in a recent conversation with a young lady, she shared with me how the relationship she had been in for a couple of years had left her perplexed and at a point in her life that she had not experienced before. She communicated that over a period time, many heated exchanges had occurred in the relationship. After such, the usual mode of operation was to superficially confront the issue and quickly allow things to go "back to normal." While this behavior had no apparent immediate implications, the truth of the matter is that over a period of time and with every occurrence, there was an accumulation of frustration, irritation, vexation, aggravation, and dissatisfaction taking place. As a result, this cyclical process had now brought her to a place of absolute fury. She realized that it was insane to expect different results if she continued to allow the same behavior. She also had come to understand that in order for her situation to change, she would need to take immediate action to begin the change process. In essence, her unhealthy state of affairs had finally helped her to realize that enough was *enough*.

This Is for You: Many of us have had instances in our lives where we've encountered people or entities that in some way or another have drawn us into a phase of acquiescence or acceptance. In fact, you may be there at this very moment. Although this way of conducting ourselves is not wrong, it is extremely problematic when we continually assume a role that jeopardizes our overall well-being. In this case, we have to ask ourselves, "How much am I willing to compromise who I am in God for the sake of love, money, career, or whatever? If where you are has caused you to lose sight of who God created you to be and what He created you to do—have you had *enough* yet? If not, what else is it going to take? Assess where you are, compared to where you want to be. Your answer may be your call to action

God's Word to You: "And it shall come to pass, when you become restless, then you shall break his yoke from your neck" (Genesis 27:40).

Day Three Journal Discovery

1. Are you sick and tired of being sick and tired? What is the cause of your weariness?

2. After realizing that enough is enough, what is your plan for resolution?

3. How will making modifications in what you allow in your life move you closer to living on purpose?

Preparation for the Test

Life is a test and this world a place of trial. Always problems—or it may be the same problem—presented to every generation in different forms.

—Winston Churchill

MY DAUGHTER RECENTLY got her driving permit. Needless to say, she was absolutely ecstatic. On the day she received it, she walked around smiling with that little laminated card in her hand as if it was going to disappear if she put it down. I even caught sporadic glimpses of her just staring at it. Her picture identification on the permit had the biggest, brightest smile I had seen in quite some time. It seemed she could not believe she had accomplished something as great as this.

In her zeal, she began to lay her vehicular dreams and visions out for me. All she could talk about was the fact that she was on her way to getting her driver's license ("license" being official permission to do a specified thing). As a result, she had already requested that her father get her a car for her sixteenth birthday. She already knew the make, model, and color of the vehicle she wanted. She had already looked far enough ahead to see herself driving to school for her junior and senior years. She knew what type of ornament she would have hanging on the rearview mirror and what kind of scent she would have tucked under the seat to keep her car fresh. When riding with others, she was very intentional about paying close attention to driving direction so that she would know exactly where she was going when it was her turn to drive. She even had made friends with the owners of the local carwash, hoping to get "the family discount" when she took her car there.

However, in all of her excitement, I noticed one thing. She never mentioned her plans for taking the driver's test. She talked about going out to drive to make good use of her permit. She talked about all she was going to do once she had a license and a car. In many of her conversations, she even threw in the fact that she would be able to help me tremendously once she was able to drive (ha, ha). Nevertheless, in all of her discussion, there was not one mention of preparing for the impending, critical evaluation to determine the presence, quality, and precision of her driving abilities. In essence, she had conceptualized the outcome she so earnestly desired, but she had not analyzed the preparation required.

Oftentimes as we speak of our dreams and visions and lay them out before God, we are so excited about the outcome that we do not recognize there may be tests associated with our requests. Therefore, because we are not thinking about the test, we fail to adequately prepare. As a result, we become discombobulated because we don't recognize it for what it is.

I remember my days growing up when I would be watching television, and in the middle of the show the screen would go to a circular symbol and a loud noise would sound. This would last for approximately sixty seconds. Because I was never prepared for what was coming, I can remember being extremely irritated by the interruption of the flow of whatever show I was watching. My only focus and concern was getting back to the program I had been viewing before all this transpired.

However, as I grew older, I came to understand the need for this occurrence. I learned that this was a test alert from the Emergency Broadcast System, which served as an emergency warning system in the United States. This system was implemented to allow the President to address the entire nation in case of an emergency. Therefore, the system was tested often through critical evaluation to ensure its functionality. The test occurred by suspending the viewing of a program and sounding an alert to get the attention of all viewers. The following message would then be communicated, "This is a test. This station is conducting a test of the Emergency Broadcast System. This is only a test." After the sixty seconds, or what seemed like infinity, the interruption ended.

We often respond to spiritual tests in the same manner. We grumble and complain about the test, but we fail to realize that going through the test is what prepares us for the real emergency. We become irritated by the interruptions they bring, and we magnify them to the degree that they seem to last for a time without end. As a result, we ask God to move it, take us out of it, or change it. We complain when it seems to be too hard and retreat when it doesn't seem to go our way.

This Is for You: To truly understand and ensure our consistent functionality, we must be willing to undergo critical evaluation for God to determine the presence, quality, and precision of our abilities to handle those issues that arise for our lives. Preparation for this requires that we submit and realize that much of what we are going through is only a test.

God's Word to You: "The refining pot is for silver and the furnace for gold, but the Lord tests the hearts" (Psalm 17:3).

Day Four Journal Discovery

1. What connections have you made between where you want to go and the preparation for tests that may be necessary to get you there?

2. How can you adequately prepare for tests you will have to face?

3. How can tests that come into your life move you closer to living on purpose?

Can You Stand the Rain?

For the man sound in body and serene of mind there is no such thing as bad weather. Every sky has its beauty, and storms which whip the blood do but make it pulse more vigorously.

—George Gissing

A PART OF my early morning routine had been to turn on the television and tune in to the local news and listen intently for the weather report. Although the local news was important, before I could take my shower, choose an outfit, or determine my hairstyle, I had to hear from the meteorologist. His report had become a vital part of my day and would often be the determining factor for my mood, appearance, and schedule. Therefore, I would brace myself when he began to talk about the forecast, concerned that the weather conditions for that day may include the prediction of rain.

Why? Because mine was the same sentiment as the childhood nursery rhyme: "Rain, rain, go away. Come again some other day." In my opinion, rain metaphorically had a sad and negative connotation in contrast to the bright and happy sunshine.

Therefore, in anticipating and then experiencing the rain, many changes took place in my life. For example, my mood would change because the gray clouds hid the sunlight and everything seemed dreary.

My appearance was impacted because my curls were going to fall and my hair was going to frizz because of the humidity. My shoes were going to get wet, so there was no need to wear the cute ones. I didn't need to go all out with an outfit because it was going to be covered up most of the day by my all-weather coat. My morning commute was going to be hectic because when it rained many people forgot that they ever knew how to drive. If by chance there was a fender-bender on the interstate, then traffic was going to come to a standstill simply because every single vehicle seemed to have to go three miles per hour just to get a look. Once in my office, I was going to be limited as to my options for lunch because I wouldn't want to go back out into the rain, unless it was absolutely necessary. So, in essence, the rain (or anticipation of it) had already ruined my day before I was barely out of bed.

However, on one occasion, in the midst of my rainy-day stupor, I was reminded of some spiritual parallels associated with rain. We have heard the old cliché that suggests, "There's got to be some rain in your life to appreciate the sunshine." But, how many of us truly take into consideration the need for rain in our lives? In the natural world, one of the primary functions of rain is to supply much-needed water to areas that would otherwise experience tremendous drought. Without rain, there would be limited vegetation and the depletion of healthy fruit. There would be stunted plant growth and insufficient harvests. If the rain were truly to go away, life for us would literally come to an end.

Our spiritual existence is often reflective of the same. The well-being of our souls can actually be measured by whether or not there is the presence or absence of spiritual rain. Isaiah 55:10–11 states:

> For as the rain comes down from heaven, and does not return there, but waters the earth, and makes it bring forth and bud, that it may give seed to the sowers and bread to the eater, so shall My word be that goes forth from My mouth; it shall not return to Me void, but it shall accomplish what I please, and it shall prosper in the thing for which I sent it.

From this perspective, rain is symbolic of the Word of God. Therefore, if we do not incorporate this form of precipitation (His Word) into our lives, we will become consumed by drought in our spirits. If we will not immerse ourselves in this rain, we will not grow, nor can we produce growth. If we completely eliminate this spiritual rain in our lives, there will be no fruit manifested from our spirits and our harvest will be bleak.

This Is for You: If I were to assume the role as a spiritual meteorologist, I believe it would be safe to say that spiritual rain (The Word) in our lives should be a welcomed part of our very existence. The question is, "Can you stand the rain?" Can you stand the times when this rain beats upon circumstances in your life that you are not ready or willing to change? Can you stand the times when this rain pours the truth on your conscience and calls you to love and forgive? Can you stand the times when this rains comes to saturate your flesh to keep you from sin? The rain in our lives is not to be avoided, but rather it should become an anticipated opportunity by which we learn the benefits of "Walking in the rain with the One we love."

God's Word to You: "All Scripture is given by inspiration of God, and is profitable for doctrine, for reproof, for correction, for instruction in righteousness, that the man of God may be complete, thoroughly equipped for every good work" (2 Timothy 3:16–17).

Day Five Journal Discovery

1. What role does rain (the Word of God) play in your life?

2. What is your plan for more "rainy days"?

3. How will incorporating more rain (The Word) in your life make you more alive and move you closer to living on purpose?

Something on the Inside

What lies behind us and what lies before us are tiny matters compared to what lies within us.

—R.W. Emerson

I HAVE HAD some horrific experiences on my personal life's journey. I have encountered situations that have impacted my life to the degree that I questioned if I would ever overcome the struggle and pain that consumed me. Two of the most devastating experiences were the loss of my father and the end of my marriage. These events left me grieving to the point of borderline insanity and angrily interrogating God as if He was on trial for reckless abandonment. I wanted to know where He was and what He was doing while all of this was going on in my life. Nevertheless, along the journey, I found inspiration through meaningful conversations, powerful sermons, and rich biblical teachings that suggested I should forget and let go of those painful occurrences that were now behind me. Instead, I should focus on all that was ahead for me.

As I changed my mind-set to reflect this way of thinking and doing, I began to receive affirmations and confirmations from others regarding my giftedness and how my future held great promise. As a result, I began to move through my pain by reciting these intentions for my life on a regular basis: "My latter days shall be greater than my former....There are great things in store for me....My best is yet to come."

However, although these things were very true, it seemed as if I was still missing an important aspect of the process. As I worked hard to forget my past, while maintaining the motivation to envision my future, I still came face-to-face with insurmountable struggles. I could not manage to wrap my spiritual mind around the concept of true victory and overcoming faith. There were issues from my past that still tripped me up. There were people from my past that still knew where my buttons were despite the fact that I was certain I had disposed of or hidden them. Therefore, I found myself constantly responding to external triggers, and I was very unstable in my emotions.

For that reason, I sought God in the midst of my frustration. In doing so, my attention was drawn to the fact that every negative experience that I had committed to putting behind me, and every positive hope that I had established for the future I believed was before me, was not as important as the work God still desired to do inside of me. In other words, I learned that it didn't matter if I had a "testimony" from my past or "gifts" for my future, if I was not willing to submit to the building of what was presently most important to God: my character.

This Is for You: Merriam-Webster defines character as "the attributes or features that make up and distinguish our moral strength and reputation." When God builds our character, He is in actuality making us distinguishably His by placing us under renovation and reconstructing the very nature of who we are. The difficult part in this building process is that God allows situations where we are wronged, scandalized, and offended as He watches for us to respond in ways that honor Him. He watches how we respond in the midst of the hurt. He watches how we respond in the midst of the anger. He watches how we respond in the midst of the frustration. He watches how we respond in the midst of the shame. He watches for signs of growth and obedience. And until we submit to His building, our past can never be a testimony for us, nor do the gifts of the future mean anything to us, if our present character can't sustain us.

God's Word to You: "And not only that, but we also glory in tribulations, knowing that tribulation produces perseverance; and perseverance, character; and character, hope" (Romans 5:3–4).

Day Six Journal Discovery

1. What are the challenges in your life you believe God is using to build character in you right now?

2. How will you respond to character-building opportunities in the future?

3. How will allowing God to build your character move you closer to living on purpose?

Check the Label

You cannot starve a man who is feeding on God's promises.

—E.C. Olsen

OVER THE YEARS, one of the things I have learned to do on a consistent basis is pamper myself. I have found it is extremely important to take the time to refill, refresh, replenish, refurbish, refuel, and any other "re" that is a necessary part of God's plan of sustainability for my life. In the process, I am also teaching my daughter to do the same. For instance, every other Saturday we join in a special treat to ourselves by going to get our hair done.

This mother-daughter bonding time consists of many valuable components. We recline side-by-side at the shampoo bowl while the conditioner sits on our hair. We also sit next to each other under the hair dryers, sharing magazines, and eating each other's snacks. This also gives us an opportunity to talk. Although no one in the salon has ever said so, I imagine our conversations are pretty loud, since we find it difficult to hear; but we choose to talk anyway.

Nevertheless, this past Saturday I made a very interesting observation. While sitting under the dryer, I watched my hairstylist make two trips to the snack basket, which is provided for all clients. This basket contained beautiful fresh fruit, a variety of bags of chips, and packs of assorted crackers all nicely arranged. On her first trip to the basket she chose a banana. I was not surprised at all by her choice because she is one of the most health-conscious people I know. However, on her second trip she picked up various packs of crackers and began to read the labels. She went from one pack to the other, intently reading the nutritional values of each. After her inquisitive search, she walked away from the basket without making any selection at all.

In watching this chain of events, I could only surmise that while she was attracted to the packs of crackers because of their appetizing appeal and inviting displays, after thoroughly evaluating the label and assessing the real contents of the crackers, she decided the temptation to indulge in them was not worth suffering the consequences because of what was really in them.

This Is for You: According to the Agricultural Utilization Research Institute, the purpose of nutrition facts labeling "is to help consumers choose more healthful diets." It tells us the daily recommended values related to what we are about to consume. It tells us how much, how little, or if there is no value in the item at all.

There are times when we are tempted by people or things that come into our lives adorned with enticing wrappers and alluringly positioned. In other words, they are appealing to the eye, and their presentation is welcoming. But, what about the label?

When you face an attractive temptation, you must ask yourself, "Is yielding to the temptation of what I see meeting the daily recommended allowance that God has established for my life?" If your answer is a definitive "no," then it is in your best interest to step away from that which entices you and make a healthier choice.

God's Word to You: "Oh taste and see that the Lord is good. Blessed is the man who trusts in Him" (Psalm 34:8).

Day Seven Journal Discovery

1. Think about the people or things that have come in and out of your life. Did you check the label before indulging? What was the impact?

2. If you had checked the label first, in what way(s) would your experiences have been different?

3. In the future, what will be the value of checking labels and how will doing so move you closer to living on purpose?

Can I Get a Boost?

—⚬—

Never give in, never give in, never, never, never, never—in nothing, great or small, large or petty—never give in except to convictions of honour and good sense.

—Winston Churchill

MY SON BEGAN his first year of college in mid-August. Although he was able to take many items with him from home, he was not able to take his car. As a result, it had been sitting in the garage undisturbed until he came home for Labor Day weekend. Needless to say, before returning home he had already formulated plans for his weekend—where he was going to go, who he was going to see, and errands he was going to run.

When he arrived home on Friday, he brought with him a huge bag of laundry and dropped it in the laundry room, lovingly greeted everyone, chit-chatted for a few minutes, briefly went over his agenda with me, then grabbed his keys, and headed for the garage. He enthusiastically jumped into his car with great expectation that he was going to be on his way to fulfilling his plans. But, much to his disappointment, when he put his key in the ignition, his car would not start. He tried several times, growing more and more frustrated with every failed attempt. Finally, he got out of his car after reaching an extreme height of aggravation and began agonizing over the fact that, because of a dead battery, he wouldn't be able to do all that he had set out to accomplish.

As I observed his agitation and rapidly growing anger, I interjected, "Honey, why don't you just call someone for a boost?" At that moment, it was as if the light bulb on the top of his head came on and with it a smile that suggested, "Why didn't I think of that?" Nevertheless, he took immediate action. He called a mechanic he knew who had the equipment he needed to give his car a boost. Once it was charged enough to start, he was given the following directions:

- Drive long enough to let the charging system do its work.
- Drive at a constant speed.
- Turn off all unnecessary accessories such as the radio, air conditioner, etc.

With a running car and directions to keep it going, he set out to fulfill the plans he had made.

There was an awesome lesson in this incident for me. There are times when we allow the gifts that God has given us to sit inactive long enough for our spiritual batteries to die. We keep these spiritual gifts stored in our personal garages while we go off in other directions to do other things. However, when we return and are in need of those gifts to facilitate our plans, because we have not been igniting them on a regular basis, there is not enough power for them to perform. Much like a battery, if our gifts are not consistently used, then power drainage will occur. As a result, we become extremely disappointed, frustrated, and aggravated because of multiple failed attempts and our ultimate inability to move.

This Is for You: You possess gifts that God has given you to carry you to your purpose and destination. How, and in what areas, have you allowed those gifts to sit idle in your life to the degree you have lost the power to get started? As you identify those areas, it's time for you to go into action. Ask God in prayer to move you out of the place of disappointment, frustration, and aggravation, and to give you the boost (power) you need to get your engine ignited and then:

- Move forward long enough to let your charging gifts do their work.
- Keep going at a consistent speed, versus starting and stopping again.
- Turn off everything that is an unnecessary accessory in your life.

After all, what good does it do you to have the vehicles if you are not using them to take you where God has planned for you to go?

God's Word to You: "Therefore I remind you to stir up the gift of God which is in you" (2 Timothy 1:6).

Day Eight Journal Discovery

1. What gifts have you allowed to lie dormant in your life? What has been the impact of this inactivity?

2. What will you do to reignite your gifts and to use them for the purpose for which God gave them to you?

3. How do you see yourself using your rejuvenated gifts to move you closer to living on purpose?

The Power of Purpose

Desire accomplished is sweet to the soul.

—Proverbs 13:19

I'VE HAD CONVERSATIONS with a number of women who expressed personal discontent and a desire to move in a new direction, go to the next level, begin a new journey, or make life-changes. Many of them didn't know how to name it or what to call it; they just knew that where they were wasn't where they wanted to be. They had grown weary of "business as usual," and the status quo just was not meeting a much deeper need. Daily routines had become draining and lacked purpose and vision. In addition, they lacked a sense of peace, balance, and overall well-being. It seemed as if a general sense of unsettling hovered over their lives and could not be shaken.

As we shared with each other, I could feel the load of these women. As a matter of fact, their discontentment resonated with my own unfulfilled state of being. In actuality, I believe our mutual disturbance is what drew me to them and them to me at that time. Among us was a general consensus that we all had developed a longing in our spirits to do more and be more—not in a busy way, but in a way that moved us out of the mundane, habitual ruts of life and into a place of sustainable fulfillment. Although at different levels and degrees, we all seemed to be grieving the loss of our peace and contentment, while maintaining a desperate need to find a way to move forward.

As a result of these conversations, I knew that I needed to take some sort of action if I was going to move beyond this place. Therefore, I began my own personal search. I sought the face of God concerning those things that were weighing heavily on my own heart. I laid my frustration, my fatigue, my weightiness, my confusion, my attitude, and my anxiety all at His feet. I acknowledged where I was and that I lacked direction, and I simply prayed, "Father, please show me which way to go."

Just as I had asked—He began to place situations in my life to show me the value of my gifts and all He had invested in me. He began to open doors of opportunity where my gifts could be used to bring Him glory. Finally, He revealed to me that the real longing I had experienced in my soul was actually His vehicle to move me to a true place of *purposeful* living. God reminded me that I, along with every other woman I had spoken to, had been created with purpose—for purpose—on purpose. In other words, God had fashioned each of us with an outcome that He intended and planned for our lives. Moreover, the power to transform our discontented state of being is available to each of us if only we will understand and pursuing this purpose.

This Is for You: Do you know what it means to live your life on purpose? Have you earnestly desired and found opportunities to consistently use your God-given gifts, talents, and abilities in a way that brings you a sense of fulfillment and brings God glory? Are you still waking up each morning and saying to yourself, "One day I'm going to …" Do you think if you wait long enough your purpose will find you?

Depending on how you answered these questions, you are either experiencing the joys of purposeful living or there is a "purpose problem." Your gifts have been given to you to facilitate your purpose. They cannot be fully functional without a purpose for their use. Therefore, if you have not sought God for His purpose for your life, or if you have in some way deviated from His purpose for your life, I encourage you to ask Him to show you. When He reveals it to you, write it down and let your purpose fill your heart. Knowing and walking in your purpose is the road map and fuel for your journey here on earth. Where you want to go is too important for you not to have the directions or gas to get you there.

God's Word to You: "May He grant you according to your heart's desire, And fulfill all your purpose" (Psalms 20:4).

Day Nine Journal Discovery

1. Describe your desire to go to the next dimension in your life.

2. What has hindered you from moving from where you are to the place you desire to be?

3. What are the immediate changes you need to make in your life to move you closer to living on purpose?

Building Bridges

You have to count on living every single day in a way you believe will make you feel good about your life so that if it were over tomorrow, you'd be content with yourself.

—Jane Seymour

I HAVE BEEN blessed with two beautiful nieces, ages six and one. It has been fascinating to watch the development of their personalities, demeanor, and dispositions. However, I have been most intrigued by the "adult-like" nature of the six-year-old. In fact, in the middle of conversations with her, I have had to remind myself that she really is only six. She has amused our family with quick-witted responses and stories that would lead you to believe that she had a personal writer and coach for her material.

Most recently, my sister was in the middle of correcting my niece regarding what was deemed as inappropriate behavior. During the lecture, my niece stood as she listened attentively to her mother's words. However, after a lengthy discourse and the recognition that her actions had caused my sister apparent irritation and frustration, my niece interjected the following words of advice: "Mom…just build a bridge and get over it." While this was an extremely inappropriate response, and I am certainly not endorsing it, the point of my niece's comment is worth grasping.

As I reflected on those words, I drew the conclusion that in many instances in our lives there is a very real need for us to build our own bridges and get over them. Webster defines a bridge as, "A structure providing passage over a gap or barrier, allowing people to cross over obstacles." On our personal journeys, we encounter various gaps or interruptions in our lives. It could be a gap in a relationship, a gap in finances, a gap in health, or even gaps in our own sense of purpose or well-being. Whatever the case, these gaps have ultimately hindered us from getting to the side of life where God has destined for us to be. Oftentimes, the gaps, barriers, and obstacles have appeared to be insurmountable. We have looked at them and declared, "I don't know how I am going to get over this." As a result of our own words and our mind-set of defeat, we have become so overwhelmed and tired; we have forgotten to simply build a bridge.

This Is for You: To build your bridge means that you must involve yourself in constructing a structure that provides you passage over gaps, barriers, and obstacles in your life. For me, that building process began with the recognition that I could not stay where I was. I could not allow the gaps, barriers, or obstacles to dictate how far I would make it on my journey and whether or not I would reach my destiny. Therefore, I developed an intestinal fortitude that suggested, "I am going to get to the other side of this situation one way or another." So it just made sense for me to work toward constructing or reconstructing mechanisms in my life that would allow me to pass over those things that otherwise would still be holding me back.

The primary tool in my building process is the Word of God. When faced with life's interruptions and hindrances, I have used God's Word to help me pass over the situations and circumstances that have impeded my progress. I have had to use the building blocks found in the Word of God to help me make it through the times I wanted to call it quits. I had to use these blocks to help me hold my head up in the midst of my enemies. I had to use these building blocks to help me forgive those I perceived to be unforgivable and to love those I felt were unlovable.

I had to build block by block until I had been fully equipped to build my bridge.

The choice is yours too—to rely upon the truths of God's Word to transport you to your destination, or to give up and place a sign over your life that reads, "Not Accessible, Bridge Out."

God's Word to You: "Your word is a lamp to my feet and a light to my path" (Psalm 119:105).

Day Ten Journal Discovery

1. What are those areas in your life that you know you need to "get over"?

2. What is your plan for constructing or reconstructing ways to get you to the other side of these areas?

3. What internal changes do you have to make in order to maintain your bridge and to move you closer to living on purpose?

Part II

My Mind

F.A.I.T.H.

Faith is not belief. Belief is passive. Faith is active. It is wisdom which passes inevitably into action.

—Edith Hamilton

AS I LOOK back over my life, I can recall many experiences that have impacted my journey toward living on purpose. I have had ups and downs, highs and lows, and ebbs and flows. In life, I have traveled through the good, the bad, and the ugly. But one of the most difficult times in my life offered me a hidden treasure of wisdom and became the catalyst for a life-changing encounter that literally transformed my life.

Here is my story:

I walked into the bathroom to start the process for my bubble bath. Feeling as if my heart had been ripped out of my chest, stepped on, and placed back inside, I grabbed my note pad and my Bible. I believed this was my only lifeline and way out of the dejection, discouragement, and depression in which I was drowning. As I settled into the water, it took every fiber left of my being not to put my head under in an attempt to end my misery.

However, I held onto everything I ever believed about God and instead spoke quietly to Him out of my broken heart. "Father, I need a message from you." I sat quietly and waited. There was no answer. "Father, I really need to hear from you." The tears begin to flow. "If I don't hear from you, I am not going to make it." My pain moved up to my throat and blocked any other words I could have possibly said out loud. So, I just sat, cried, and waited.

After a time of being still, the Holy Spirit inspired my heart to turn my Bible to Hebrews 11:1. I read the words, "Now faith is the substance of things hoped for, the evidence of things not seen." I pondered the scripture for a moment. Then, my response to what I had just read was heated and charged with attitude. "God, I know that already—can you please give me something I don't already know—something other than a definition of faith?"

I thought about how I had learned that scripture in vacation Bible school when I was a little girl. Surely I should be able to get a message from the omnipotent, omniscient, omnipresent, and almighty God—something that was more meaningful than what seemed a clichéd Sunday school memory verse.

Although angered from my tantrum with God and wallowing in my private pity party, I still waited for something—anything that would offer me some respite for my soul. Finally, after what seemed to be an eternity, I heard in a still small voice: "That is not a definition of faith. That is a description of faith. I am going to give you your own personal definition of faith." With great anticipation I held my pen and note pad in my hand. The Holy Spirit led me to write the letters F.A.I. T. H. on my paper. While staring at this inscription, I heard the Spirit say, "Here is your personal definition of faith," and I wrote: *Fully Allow It To Happen.* These words seemed to leap off the page into my chest as a soothing medicine to my aching heart and spirit. From that definition, He allowed me to see that there was no "It" that had taken place in my life that He was not aware of, nor would there ever be. Not only did He know my "It," but also He desired to bring me through it and deliver me from it. He helped me to recognize that every "It" I had faced and would ever face had been completed in Jesus on the cross when He said, "It is finished." So my responsibility was to fully allow "It," the completed work, to happen.

This Is for You: What "It" are you facing in your life that has impeded your progress toward living on purpose? It could be a broken heart, a shattered dream, or a loss of hope or desire. It could be a wrong or unhealthy relationship, or a lack of direction for a given area of your life. It could be your weariness with the process that God is taking you through. It could be your eagerness to experience the next thing that God has for you. It could be recurring issues that you just can't seem to rid yourself of or issues you just don't want to let go. Whatever the case may be, God has called you to a place to walk by F. A. I. T.H. Can you trust Him with your "It"? Because, without *Fully Allowing It To Happen,* it is impossible to please Him.

God's Word to You: "The just shall live by faith" (Habakkuk 2:4).

Day Eleven Journal Discovery

1. What is the "It" in your life that you need to entrust to God?

2. What hindrances or obstacles do you have to overcome in order to fully surrender your "It" to God?

3. How can "Fully Allowing It To Happen" move you closer to living on purpose?

Live Forward

I walk slowly, but I never walk backward.
—Attributed to Abraham Lincoln

A FEW WEEKENDS ago, I was on my way to the shopping center to meet my cousin for brunch. As I drove through several neighborhoods onto the main road to the shopping center, I could vaguely hear a horn blowing behind me. Nevertheless, I kept looking straight ahead. After about sixty seconds of sporadic horn-blowing, out of the corner of my eye I could see an SUV pull from behind me and move up beside me. Still looking ahead, I caught a quick glimpse of the person driving the vehicle. This person put the window down and began waving—trying to get me to look in her direction. However, the more this person tried, the more I continued looking ahead.

One of the reasons for my insistence on staying focused on the road in front of me was because I was determined not to be distracted by some person trying to get my attention, possibly to offer some gesture or comment that I would not appreciate…if you know what I mean. Secondly, to take my eyes off the road to examine the source of the noisy horn behind me, even for a split second, could have resulted in a serious accident. My focus was simply to get to the shopping center to accomplish the purpose for which I had set out.

After the continuous attempts to break my resolute concentration did not work, my cell phone rang. When I answered, the voice on the other end said, "I can't believe after all of that, I can't get you to look at me." Immediately I looked over into the SUV that was now stopped beside me at a traffic light. I quickly realized that it was an old acquaintance that I had not seen in quite some time.

As I reflected on this event, I saw the spiritual connection. There are times in our lives when metaphorical vehicles carrying people, situations, and circumstances can come up behind us in an attempt to get our attention. These vehicles are often driven by something or someone familiar to us—an old acquaintance that perhaps we have not seen in a while. Many times the vehicles are blowing noisy horns from our past trying to get us to remember those things we once resolved to leave behind us. The vehicles may also pull up beside us waving familiar issues in our face in an effort to deter us from our future. By any means necessary, the vehicles come to entice us to change our direction and to distract us from the road that lies ahead—to get us to look away, if even for a moment.

This Is for You: Who or what has been driving up behind you? What have you been looking at in your rearview mirror? There are times when we all have to ask ourselves these questions. As past issues come up behind us (people, hurts, relationships, or any other issue), we have a choice as to whether or not we are going to look in that direction. So what if the noise of the past seems loud? So what if there are distractions that are seemingly waving you down? I suggest you forget about it.

If you don't, are you really going to appreciate what you find if you move your eyes from looking forward? How safe will you be traveling on your journey if you are looking backwards while trying to move forward at the same time? What lengths are you willing to go to in order to avoid the fatalities of a serious accident due to an inability to stay focused on those things which are ahead? The goal in keeping your eyes forward is really simple—you just want to get to where you're going for the purpose that God has ordained. Therefore, *remember* to *forget* those things that are behind you. Make a commitment to live forward today.

God's Word to You: "Brethren, I do not count myself to have apprehended; but one thing I do, forgetting those things which are behind and reaching forward to those things which are ahead" (Philippians 3:13).

Day Twelve Journal Discovery

1. How has your past been a distraction to you living your life forward? Be specific.

2. If you change your focus, what will you be able to accomplish?

3. What steps will you take to live your life forward as you move closer to living on purpose?

Unlimited Re-Source

*There is something in the nature of things which the mind of men,
which reason, which human power cannot effect, and certainly
that which produces this must be better than man. What can this
be but God?*

—Cicero

FOR A COUPLE of years, a portion of my life's work was dedicated to
providing consulting and technical assistance to non-profit organizations.
During this time, I was afforded the opportunity to meet one-on-one
with executive directors, boards of directors, and executive staff. In
an effort to create a profile for these clients, one of the questions I
consistently asked was, "What is your greatest challenge to successful and
sustainable programmatic implementation?" Without fail, the number
one response was "limited resources." Each organizational leader talked
about the challenges of trying to operate programs on an ongoing basis
when the revenue, assets, and capital were in limited supply. For many,
year after year, the life span of the organization was solely dependent
upon accessing the next source of funding or provision.

Today, as I recall the plight of many of these organizations, I am also
aware that many of us live our spiritual lives in the same manner—with
very limited or no resources at all. In essence, we are going about our

day-to-day activities faced with the challenges of operating on an ongoing basis when the supply of what we need seems beyond our grasp. Allow me to explain:

The *American Heritage Dictionary* defines "source" as, "One that causes, creates, or initiates." Moreover, the prefix "re" means "again or anew." In this context, a (re)source is one that causes, creates, or initiates again or anew.

God is our Source. He causes, creates, initiates, and makes His provisions for our lives again and again and anew every day. Therefore, if we lack spiritually, we are actually operating without truly accessing the One who causes, creates, or initiates every single thing we need for the success and sustainability of our lives.

It is important to understand that people, jobs, bank accounts, stocks, bonds, or other investment portfolios are not our Source. God simply Re-Sources Himself in and through these entities as a means of funneling His provisions to us. For instance, He will Re-Source Himself through people and cause them to give to us in ways we could never have imagined. He will Re-Source Himself through our jobs and create a means by which our needs are met abundantly, above all that we can ask or think. He will Re-Source Himself in our financial matters and initiate blessings that pour out on us to overflow. He is also a Re-Source in our health, a Re-Source in our minds, a Re-Source in our will, a Re-Source in our emotions, a Re-Source in our relationships; He is a Re-Source in whatever we need Him to be.

I have learned that every blessing I receive is God's Re-Source to me. Therefore, I am not concerned about living a life of limited blessings. Nor am I concerned about my personal success or sustainability. I depend solely on The Source to cause, create, and initiate provisions for me in every area of my life and again and again and anew in unlimited supply. As a result, I put all my trust in Him and consistently acknowledge Him as Jehovah Jireh—The God Who Provides.

This Is for You: Be honest with yourself. Who or what have you consistently looked to as your source? Maybe you are like me. There was a time in my life when I honestly believed that my blessings were predicated on someone supplying my needs for me. Therefore, I resorted to trying to please that person so that what I perceived to be "blessings" would not be cut off or taken away. But in actuality, those pseudo-blessings were not in God's plan for me anyway. In fact, they were hindering the good things He had in store for me. My responsibility was to acknowledge the one and only Re-Source as the supplier of ALL my needs.

God's Word to You: "And my God shall supply all your need according to His riches in glory by Christ Jesus" (Philippians 4:19).

Day Thirteen Journal Discovery

1. In what areas of your life have you not acknowledged God as your source and instead looked to people or things as your source?

2. In reflection, how have you seen God Re-Sourcing Himself in your life?

3. What commitments will you make to consistently see God as your ultimate Re-Source as you move closer to living on purpose?

Oops—I Lost My Balance

Problems arise in that one has to find a balance between what people need from you and what you need for yourself.

—Jessye Norman

WHEN I WAS a little girl, one of the many activities that my playmates and I created to entertain ourselves was to spin around in a circle as fast as we could to see which one of us would fall first. We would all begin at the same time and keep going until we all fell. Ironically, we very seldom declared a winner for each round, because we were so busy trying to come out of our state of dysfunction and regain our composure so we could get up and begin spinning again. As I reflect back on those times, I am amazed and fascinated by the fact that we found so much humor and fun in losing our balance.

On the contrary, just recently I was lying in front of the fireplace in the family room of my mother's home. I got up hurriedly to walk into the other room, and things in my head and in the room began to spin. Before I knew it, I was stumblingly back and forth. After several steps in many directions, I finally fell against the coffee table, breaking my fall. I had completely lost my balance. Others in the room assisted me as they made sure I was all right. Needless to say, I did not find it humorous or fun. In fact, it was very painful, not to mention extremely embarrassing.

In life we can experience periods of time when it seems as though we have lost our balance. In this context, "balance" is defined as, "A stable mental or psychological state; emotional stability." Just like the spinning room in the incident in my mother's family room, the times when I have lost my mental, psychological, and/or emotional balance, I have also felt the horrendous impact of the loss of self-control, and many areas of my life became dysfunctional. As a result, I stumbled in many directions. I was perplexed by indecision and could not focus long enough to see my way. If I did manage to stumble into something in the midst of my dizziness, it was usually something to break my fall, but it also hurt me in the process. Why? Because being off balance made me vulnerable to anything that wound up in my path.

This Is for You: We face a number of things in life that can cause us to become unbalanced. However, according to *The American Heritage Science Dictionary*, to have balance or equilibrium there has to be, "A condition in which all acting influences are cancelled by other acting influences, resulting in a stable or unchanging system." Therefore, our challenge becomes finding ways to create and maintain the condition we need to remain balanced. So then the questions become: How do we cancel acting influences in or lives that cause us to malfunction? How do we eliminate the stressors that plague us with instability? How do we tackle exhaustion and the energy drain that cause a chemical shift in our minds to the degree we swing from mood to mood? How do we identify internal and external triggers that cause us to respond in ways that later cause regret and sorrow, ultimately leading to an emotional shut-down? How do we denounce negative thoughts and feelings that bombard our spirit and lead us into a state of depression? How do we release old wounds from our past that have held our hearts in captivity far too long? How do we learn the risks associated with giving too much of ourselves away and having nothing left for our own survival?

Maxwell Maltz once stated, "Man maintains his balance, poise, and sense of security only as he is moving." In order for us to maintain a stable or unchanging system, we must keep moving. We must move beyond those things that keep us disoriented and discombobulated. We must move to a place of total surrender to the One who is able to keep us from falling. We must give Him our minds, our hearts, and our hands. Think about it—it's really difficult to lose your balance while you have Someone holding you up.

God's Word to You: "Now unto Him who is able to keep you from stumbling, and present you faultless before the presence of His glory with exceeding joy" (Jude 2).

Day Fourteen Journal Discovery

1. Write an honest assessment of your life's balance or lack there of at this very moment.

2. What steps of surrender can you take to bring your life into the personal balance that gives you an overall sense of well-being?

3. How will creating balance in your life move you closer to living on purpose?

Fresh Fruit

~❧❧◯

What we do belongs to what we are; and what we are is what becomes of us.

—Henry Van Dyke

MY FAVORITE SEASON of the year is summer. Besides the warm weather, beautiful flowers, and my ability to wear sandals and no pantyhose, summer is the season for my favorite fruits. I absolutely love peaches, plums, nectarines, strawberries, watermelon, and cantaloupe. However, this year I have been a bit challenged in consistently finding good fresh fruit. I tried produce departments in various supermarkets throughout the city.

Upon entering the produce section, I was very enticed by the fruit's vibrant colors and sweet aroma. Because of its appearance, I could hardly wait to get home to taste it. However, much to my dismay, the fruit that had drawn my attention and led me to believe that it would serve as a gastronomical delight, after one bite, left me extremely disappointed. This fruit would be dry, hard on the inside, too ripe, too bitter, or have no taste at all—just no good.

Before resolving that I would not return to this store's produce department because of my many disappointing attempts to find the best fruit, I asked an attendant working in the produce section what the problem was with the fruit. He explained to me that the fruit was not as good this season due to damage the storms and harsh weather had caused in the previous seasons. Hurricanes and winter ice had caused harm at the core of the internal components that were responsible for the fruit's complete development. Therefore, there was nothing anyone could do to help the fruit that was on display, because the damage had already been done.

And it struck me: Many times in our lives we have looked for the good fruit in others. We look for love, joy, peace, longsuffering, kindness, goodness, faithfulness, gentleness, and self-control. We want it to be ripe, sweet, and satisfying to our taste. What we fail to realize is that the fruit we are expecting to see in others is often not what it could be because of the damage that has been done to it by storms and harsh weather from previous life's seasons. Therefore, it is unrealistic of us to expect that we are going to get anything from that person other than what has been displayed in front of us.

Likewise, we have to ask ourselves, what do others find when they inspect our fruit? Are we able to attract them with our vibrant colors when they see our devotion to God through our love, joy, and peace? Do we draw them with our sweet aroma by demonstrating longsuffering, kindness, and goodness? Do we satisfy their taste through our actions of faithfulness, gentleness, and self-control? Or, do we give the appearance of all these things, and leave them disillusioned by how dry we are, how hard we are, and how bitter we are, or because we have no taste at all? If we are fruitful in appearance only, we must plan to recover from the storm and harsh weather damage from previous seasons in our lives. It's time to give attention to our personal produce departments.

This Is for You: Have you allowed previous seasons to affect the fruit that is being produced in your life? Only the Holy Spirit can produce fresh fruit that is pleasing to God and fruit that will remain. It cannot be produced by our own efforts. The fruit of the Spirit is *singular*—there is no separation. The Holy Spirit does not produce love without joy and peace. He does not produce longsuffering without kindness and goodness. He does not make you gentle with self-control and not call you to be faithful. In essence, He does not give us one part without the others. When He produces fruit in us, He makes us whole. It is therefore our responsibility not to allow our seasons of storms and harsh weather to damage or fragment what He has produced. When God inspects your fruit, will He stamp it, "Fresh"?

God's Word to You: "But the fruit of the Spirit is love, joy, peace, longsuffering, kindness, goodness, faithfulness, gentleness, self-control. Against such there is no law" (Galatians 5:22–23).

Day Fifteen Journal Discovery

1. What do you find when you inspect the fruit that is being produced in your life?

2. In reflection, how has the manifestation of your fruit impacted others?

3. How can you truly take on the fruit of the Spirit and allow it to move you closer to living on purpose?

What Really Matters?

~⁂

*What you have been is not important. What really counts in your
life is what you are reaching for, what you are becoming.*

—Eric Butterworth

HAVE YOU STOPPED to listen to the responses you get when you ask
others how they're doing? The customary responses are, "fine," "good,"
or "great." However, most recently I have noticed a response that has
become more and more common, especially among women, and this is,
"*busy*." Moreover, the person giving this response often says it as if a big
"WW" (for Wonder Woman) is emblazoned across her chest. But when
you really stop to think about it, what kind of response is "busy"?

Busy is defined as, "Engaged in or sustaining much activity; cluttered
with detail to the point of being distracting." Personally, when I look at
this definition, it seems to suggest a level of energy required that I am
certain I don't want to maintain. If I am always engaged in or trying to
sustain much activity, then what is my state of well-being? If my life is
cluttered with detail to the point of being distracting, then what impact
am I having on others?

In a conversation with a dear friend of mine, she stated, "In all our
busyness, what problems are we solving?" Is wearing our busyness like a
badge of "Super Strength" worth missing out on the peace that God has

called us to? Is filling our days with meetings, tasks, and appointments worth exhausting our energy to the degree that we have little to give to the ones around us that need it the most? Is focusing our attention on doing more, being more, and achieving more worth the busyness if we are working ourselves out of the plans God has for our lives?

This Is for You: How have we allowed time to manage us instead of us managing our time? In considering the tasks that we have allowed to consume our lives, we need to ask ourselves at the end of the day, "How important to God is it?" Ask yourself, "If I am unwilling to cease from my busyness, am I prepared for all it will cost me?" This choice really does matter.

God's Word to You: "For what profit is it to a man if he gains the whole world, and loses his own soul?" (Matthew 16:26).

Day Sixteen Journal Discovery

1. When you stop to assess your busy schedule, what aspects of it are most important?

2. From your assessment, what aspect of your busyness do you perceive as being important to God?

3. What adjustments are you willing to make in your schedule to insure that you are doing what is most important to God and what will move you closer to living on purpose?

How's the View up There?

Though we can't always see it at the time, if we look upon events with some perspective, we see things always happen for our best interests. We are always being guided in a way better than we know ourselves.

—Swami Satchidananda

MY DAUGHTER AND I recently took a vacation, and we stayed in a luxurious room on the twelfth floor of a beautiful hotel. The view from our room's large window was absolutely breathtaking. We could see botanically landscaped grounds, elegant fountains, pristine pools, immaculate golf courses, and a large portion of the picturesque city. The vantage point from twelve stories high offered us magnificent clarity, optimal vision, and beauty beyond compare. We also experienced a sense of peace and well-being, all because of what we were able to see.

However, as we prepared to tour the city and then walked outside, our view changed completely. While standing in the midst of what we had seen from a higher position, it simply did not look the same. Our sight was now limited and obstructed by other obstacles on the ground. Therefore, we experienced an inability to see at any great distance, and the beauty of our surroundings was hidden. With this diminished vision, it was more difficult to appreciate enthusiastically what was around us, simply because we could not see.

This Is for You: How is the view from where you are? Are you seeing from up high or down low? Are there situations or circumstances that have blocked your vision? When we lose our ability to see or even think at a higher level, we forfeit the peace and well-being God has for us. These barriers block our view and hinder our vision to the degree we lose our motivation to see beyond where we are. During these times, we are unable to find our passion and gratitude for the beauty that is present around us.

Although there are times when we are tempted to look at our problems or an issue from a ground-level perspective, doing so completely changes our outlook on life. However, if we are going to fulfill the vision God has for us, it is imperative that we maintain a viewpoint from above—above our conditions, above our state of affairs, above the opinions of others, above anything that comes to distract or hinder our view. When we lower our view, we change our life. Is what you see right now worth looking at?

God's Word to You: "Set your mind on things above; not on things on the earth" (Colossians 3:2).

Day Seventeen Journal Discovery

1. How has your present view or perspective impacted your vision for your life?

2. When you encounter issues or situations in your life, do you look up high or down low? What are the results of choosing this view?

3. How will adjusting your view move you closer to living on purpose?

I Can't Find My Keys

In oneself lies the whole world; and if you know how to look and learn, the door is there and the key is in your hand. Nobody on earth can give you either the key or the door to open, except yourself.

—J. Krishnamurti

I WAS RECENTLY on my way to my office when I received a call with a frantic voice on the other end. "Mom, I can't find my house key." Immediately, I began asking questions to assist my daughter in back-tracking her steps to determine where her key could have been misplaced. With every question I asked came the response, "I looked there already." At the end of this exhaustive process, I told her that she would just have to wait after school until I could get there to pick her up. I told her I loved her and ended the call. However, after really thinking about the situation, I came to the realization that her lost key had set in motion a set of circumstances that had changed the course of the day for both of us.

According to *The American Heritage Dictionary*, "a key is defined as a device used for opening and locking something." In other words, keys provide access or security for many things. Therefore, the loss of my daughter's key was detrimental. Because of a lost key, she had been denied access to a place in which she was previously entitled to enter.

Moreover, the security of our home was now at risk because of the possibility that the key could have fallen into the wrong hands. Also, I was now put in a position to have to alter my schedule and direction in response to her loss.

In reflection, the spiritual parallel was eye-opening. Many of us have lost our keys to the life for which God has destined us. As a result, we have been denied access to those things we are entitled to based upon who He created us to be. Therefore, we have no devices to open doors of opportunity that have been set before us. We have no devices to lock areas in which no access should be granted. What's worse, our lost keys have jeopardized the security of our future. In addition, those closest to us have been put into positions to alter their life's direction because of the need to accommodate our misplacement.

This Is for You: On your spiritual journey and mine, keys represent the authority or power God has given us to open and close or access and secure purposeful living. If we find ourselves in situations where our keys are not in use or cannot be found, then we are limiting our access to an abundant life. Imagine that the plans and purposes of God for us have been stored up in a treasure chest. Is it realistic to expect that we can access that treasure if we have no devices (authority or power) to do so?

It's time to begin your treasure hunt. Ask for God's guidance in assisting you in finding your keys.

God's Word to You: "And I will give you the keys of the kingdom of heaven, and whatever you bind on earth, will be bound in heaven, and whatever you loose on earth will be loosed in heaven" (Matthew 16:19).

Day Eighteen Journal Discovery

1. Have you misplaced your keys? If so, how has it impacted your life?

2. Who or what can you depend on to help you find your keys? How?

3. How will finding and using your keys move you closer to living on purpose?

No Dumping Allowed

The trouble with having an open mind, of course, is that people will insist on coming along and trying to put things in it.

—Terry Pratchett

DURING A SATURDAY excursion with my mother, we decided to go into one of our favorite fast food restaurants to have a chicken sandwich for lunch. We ordered, took our seats, engaged in good conversation, and began eating our meal. While we were sitting there, one of the employees came and began the process of replacing a trash bag in a nearby receptacle that had been filled to overflowing. After struggling for a few seconds to free the bulging bag, she loaded it onto a cart, put a fresh bag in the receptacle, and took the old trash away. My mother and I completed our meals and prepared to leave. I gathered my trash and my mother's trash, piled it all on one tray, dumped it into the new trash bag, and headed out to continue our activities.

After that day, I gave no further thought to that particular event until most recently. I was having a conversation with a young woman who works in ministry. She talked about the fatigue she was beginning to experience as a result of listening to the cares, problems, concerns, issues, situations, and circumstances of others. At first, she took pleasure in hearing information and offering her advice and guidance. She believed that she was offering godly wisdom and sound teaching that would motivate these individuals toward positive results. However, after a period of time, something began to happen. Many of the people with whom she was sharing her knowledge, instruction, and personal experiences were consistently coming back to her without having made any movement or action toward obtaining positive results. Upon questioning these individuals regarding what had been discussed during their times of counsel, she found that they had done absolutely nothing with the information she had shared. However, many of them were still coming back to her for more.

Sensing her extreme frustration, I immediately recalled the events that transpired at lunch that day with my mother. It seems that just like the trash bag the young woman in the restaurant struggled with, this young woman was struggling with her own metaphorical trash bag. It had been filled to capacity, and she literally felt she had no room to receive anything else. Not only was her bag filled to the point of bursting, but the same people that had been responsible for filling it were still coming back to put more on top of what had already been deposited. What's worse, none of these "depositors" in this young woman's life had given any thought to what was happening to their trash after they dumped it on her.

This Is for You: Think about trash for a moment. Now, I am certainly not suggesting that when people come to us with information, troubles, worries, or the like, that what they share should be considered trash. However, when suggestions are given regarding how to best handle the situations and there are no actions taken, the pearls of wisdom are disregarded, and there is no progression toward change. In these cases, what we have received from others becomes a worthless, useless, unwanted waste of our time—it becomes trash.

For many of us, it is time to put up a "No Dumping" sign over our personal receptacles. It is not in our best interest, nor does it enhance our overall well-being, for us to continue to accept the rubbish brought to us by others. We are not shutting down to hearing the legitimate concerns of those who want to move forward, see a change, and go to the next level. However, we are closing the doors to those who are just looking for someone on which to dump.

God's Word to You: "Then they will call to me but I will not answer; they will look for me but will not find me. Since they hated knowledge and did not choose to fear the LORD" (Proverbs 1:28–29).

Day Nineteen Journal Discovery

1. Identify those who have consistently brought problems and issues to you with no intention to modify their situation. How have you handled this matter?

2. What are some ways you can confront these people or this person in the future to avoid the negative impact of being "dumped" on?

3. How will giving yourself permission to say "no" to listening to those who have no plan to move forward move you closer to living on purpose?

I Changed My Mind

Whatever you hold in your mind will tend to occur in your life. If you continue to believe as you have always believed, you will continue to act as you have always acted. If you continue to act as you have always acted, you will continue to get what you have always gotten. If you want different results in your life or your work, all you have to do is change your mind.

—Anonymous

IN SEPTEMBER, 2007, I was invited to Augusta, Georgia as a guest speaker for New Direction Christian Center's First Annual Women's Conference. This ministry has a cutting-edge message for people who are seeking to live a Christian life in today's world. The theme of the women's conference, "Perfecting MySpace," was symbolic of this distinction.

During a conversation with Lady Searcy, the pastor's wife, she shared with me how the Holy Spirit had given her this topic and impressed upon her ways to develop this concept. Because of the craze around the world's use of technology to create MySpace pages and profiles that reveal information (fact or fiction) about who people are, she wanted women to come together to examine and explore their own inner spaces—mind, will, and emotions. Therefore, she chose three speakers to elaborate on each topic, with mine being "Perfecting My Mind." This event was planned in excellence and detail, all the way down to the thematic colors of chocolate and turquoise.

As the first speaker, I began the presentation by telling the audience that it was not my intention to insult their intelligence; but because I am a teacher at heart, I wanted to begin by giving them a definition of the mind. I shared with them that the mind is defined as, "The seat of consciousness in which thinking and feeling takes place." I explained that as women, we are known for being thinkers and feelers. We are quick to say things such as, "This is what I think." "This is how I feel." "I think you should…" "I feel like you ought to…" But, if the mind is the *seat* of consciousness where thinking and feeling takes place, then my question to you is, who or what is sitting on your seat? In other words, who or what is really on your mind?

The brain is the most complex part of the human body. This three-pound organ houses intelligence, is the interpreter of the senses, is the initiator of body movement, and is the controller of behavior. Lying in its bony shell and washed by protective fluid, the brain is the source of all qualities that define our humanity. It is actually the crown jewel of our anatomy. So then, our brains house our mentality, intuition, perception, conception, capacity, judgment, understanding, wisdom, reasoning, wit, creativity, ingenuity, and memory. But in the midst of all these things going on in our heads, we have some other things on our minds—sitting in the seats of our consciousness.

There have been many singers and songwriters who have communicated through music and lyrics that they have love, money, and even Georgia on their mind. Whatever the case may be, we have to evaluate what is really on our mind. A part of the process of walking in our God-given destiny is to acknowledge who or what is occupying a seat in our mind.

This Is for You: The Bible says in Proverbs 23:7, "As a man thinks in his heart, so is he." Therefore, the essence of who we are is found in our thought life. This happens because we accommodate what comes in to take a seat by providing entertainment for it. Let me explain. When the enemy of our souls whispers in our ear things such as, "You're nothing, and you will always be nothing," and we entertain that thought, we make it all right for those thoughts to sit down on the seat of our consciousness and take up residence in our heads. As a result we become women struggling with low self-worth.

The enemy will also tell us, "You don't have to take that. Who do they think they are talking to?" But the moment we entertain those thoughts, we offer them a seat, and we become women with a nasty disposition, willing to give any and everybody a "piece of our mind." But, I want to encourage you to keep all your pieces. Because if you get into the habit of giving your pieces away, then you will have less on your mind and that simply makes you—mindless.

When we allow negativity to permeate our minds, we open ourselves up to darkened understanding, alienation from God, ignorance of God's way, a hardened heart, and an unfeeling state. As a result, we begin to say things such as, "Oh, I don't know if I'm coming or going." "Please excuse me, my mind is bad." "I must be out of my mind." "I feel like I'm losing my mind." Why? Because those thoughts that we have allowed to take a seat have built a house that has now become a stronghold, because they have been allowed to remain.

Therefore, it is time to change our minds. We must commit to renewing our minds to the degree that they are literally changed. The thoughts from the enemy cannot continue to assault us if the circumstances he designed to destroy us are now working to perfect us. As a result, we begin to do as Philippians 4:8 says, "Whatever things are true, whatever things are noble, whatever things are just, whatever things are pure, whatever things are lovely, whatever things are of good report, if there is any virtue and if there is anything praiseworthy—think on these things."

God's Word to You: "And do not be conformed to this world, but be transformed by the renewing of your mind, that you may prove what is that good and acceptable and perfect will of God" (Romans 12:2).

Day Twenty Journal Discovery

1. What has been sitting on your seat of consciousness and resulted in a stronghold being built in your life?

2. What actions do you need to take to change your mind? How will you ensure that the changes you make remain?

3. How will maintaining a renewed mind move you closer to living on purpose?

Free To Be Me

You can chain me, you can torture me, you can even destroy this body, but you will never imprison my mind.

—Mahatma Ghandi

IN A RECENT discussion with a young woman, I asked the question, "What is an area or some areas in your life where you have seen the greatest change occur?" After pondering my inquiry for a few moments, she began to share. She stated that she had spent most of her adult life in the business of pleasing other people. She talked about her concern regarding how they felt about her, what they thought about her, and even how she could get them to care more about her. As a result, she had begun to take drastic measures to adapt herself to what she believed others wanted and expected. She changed the way she looked. She changed the way she dressed. She changed her behavior, not because she was comfortable with these changes, but because she wholeheartedly believed that these changes were necessary to please others.

As I listened intently, I could literally feel hurt rise up in my heart. I could feel my breath grow short. I could feel my eyes fill with tears. All of the sudden, her story had become my own. As she poured out from her soul, I was drawn back to a time in the days of my youth when my life mirrored all that she was describing.

I remembered a time when what I believed was being loving to another person meant and caused me to make changes in my life that were in opposition to who and what God created me to be. Because I wanted the same thing I was feeling to be reciprocated, I began to compromise myself. I traded in my well-being to try to accommodate someone else. I traded in my self-awareness and began to receive messages from someone else telling me who I was. I traded in my sense of divine security for trying to find security in another person and the things that came with that person. I traded in my peace in my effort to try to keep peace. I traded in my other meaningful relationships in an effort to be possessed solely by another. I traded in my happiness in an effort to keep another happy. I traded in my joy because I believed I didn't really need it as long as the other person maintained it.

I traded and I traded and I traded. I traded to the degree that one day I woke up, and all of me was gone. I had willingly been taken captive by the desires of another and had voluntarily placed myself in a hostage situation. When I came to my senses, my first questions was, "Who am I, and how did I get here?" In fact, this question was the beginning of my journey out of slavery.

This Is for You: *The American Heritage Dictionary* defines "free" as, "Not imprisoned or enslaved; being at liberty. Not controlled by obligation or the will of another." Where are you in "you" right now? Are there areas in your life that are being held hostage by another person, place, or thing? Are you free to be all God created you to be?

I have learned that we are never truly free until we replace the fear for that which has us bound with the perfect love of the one good Master, Jesus Christ. The old slave masters will resist: "You will never make it without me." "You need me to survive." "I am your source." But, what is the truth? John 8:32 records Jesus saying, "And you shall know (perceive, understand, recognize) the truth, and the truth shall make you free." But a little later, Jesus further clarifies what (or better, who) truth is: "I am the way and the truth and the life" (John 14:6). You see, it's not just a matter of what you know, it's Whom you know.

So, do you know the true Master for who He really is—the only one who really knows you are more than what someone else may believe you are? He knows that you are better than what you have allowed in your life—but do you believe Him? Do you know that He has the power to make changes that are in your best interest? Do you know what Jesus Christ, your Creator, says about you? Do you know what He wants for you? Do you know that you are the apple of His eye? Do you know that He made you with plans for you and a purpose unique to you? Do you know He wants you to have an abundant life in Him? Do you know He loves you beyond what is humanly comprehensible?

If you know these truths promised by the One who himself defines truth, then you know all you need to know, and you have all you need to have to be free. But more fundamentally, you know the real Person who is Truth and who truly loves you for who you are. So go ahead… what are you waiting for? He promises that His perfect love for you will drive away all fear (1 John 4:18). You only have to accept and believe in His love for you. Know the truth personally, and be free!

God's Word to You: "Therefore if the Son makes you free, you shall be free indeed" (John 8:36).

Day Twenty-One Journal Discovery

1. In an honest assessment, identify the areas of your life where there is bondage.

2. What actions do you believe you need to take based on knowing what The Truth knows about you? How prepared are you to take those actions? If you are not prepared, what is it going to take?

3. How will becoming free to be who God created you to be move you closer to living on purpose?

Part III

My Emotions

Have You Lost Weight?

None are so empty as those who are full of themselves.

—Benjamin Whichcote

OVER AN EIGHTEEN-WEEK period, my Sunday school class did a wonderful study by Cynthia Heald entitled, "Becoming a Woman of Freedom." The premise for this study was Hebrews 12:1, "Therefore we also, since we are surrounded by so great a cloud of witnesses, let us lay aside every weight, and the sin which so easily ensnares us, and let us run with endurance the race that is set before us."

As the instructor for this class, I used various teaching methods to communicate the concepts of the study in an effort to enhance application. For example, the first chapter of the study was entitled, "Laying Aside Hindrances: Running with Freedom." As a part of a class exercise, I asked for two volunteers. Two women bravely came to the front, unsure of what was about to take place. I asked the women if they would consent to running a race a few laps around the perimeter of our classroom. They both agreed. However, before I gave them the starting alert, I handed one of the women three bags. One bag had a strap and was placed on her shoulder. She held the other two bags in her hands. After she was situated with what she had been given, I marked a starting point and communicated the standard, "On your mark...get set...go!"

Both women began running as the others in the class cheered them on. Approximately thirty seconds into the run, the woman with no bags was running with ease. She was showing no signs of fatigue and apparently had plenty of energy to keep going. However, the woman with the three bags was already in trouble. She had fallen behind and could no longer keep up with the other woman. Her breathing was labored, and on many occasions she looked as if she was going to drop all she was carrying. At the point when her struggle really began to get the best of her, she began asking me, "Can I stop now?" My response was, "No, keep going." After the seventh lap, I asked both of them to stop.

The woman with no bags slowly came to a halt, a little winded, but smiling nevertheless. However, as soon as I said "stop," the woman carrying the bags dropped them immediately and reached for a chair to sit down to catch her breath. While she rested, I asked the first woman about her experience running the race. She stated that the race had been fun for her. She enjoyed the excitement and the encouragement from the others in the class. Even when she got tired, it helped her to hear the cheers of the others, and it gave her the motivation to keep going.

Conversely, when I asked the other woman about her experience, she stated that it was more difficult than she had expected. Running with the bags impacted her in ways she never would have imagined. She stated that not only was she tired, but also she really was not mindful of the cheers from the others in the class because she was so preoccupied by the discomfort she was experiencing while focusing on not dropping her bags. She also stated that she grew impatient with me because no matter how many times she asked if she could stop, I said no. It was as if I was fully aware of her struggle and simply chose to ignore it.

After hearing her comments, I asked her to open each one of her bags. She was amazed by what she found. Inside each bag was a ten pound weight. Also, attached to the weights were words such as *envy, strife, jealousy, gossip, lust, greed, unforgiveness, anger, bitterness, revenge, rebellion, hatred, distrust, resentment, gluttony, disobedience,* and many others. In essence, she had been trying to run her race carrying all these things. What was more interesting, during the time she was running her race, she only asked if she could quit. She never asked if she could lay her bags down.

The parallels to our spiritual race were clear. The Christian life is likened to a race. We are running toward a finish in Christ that will bring glory to the Father. We are to run our race freely and without hindrances. However, when we begin to take on things that weigh us down, our race is drastically affected. We become tired and begin to lose our focus. Because of the pressure mentally, physically, and emotionally, we become disengaged from the encouragement of the Word of God that keeps us motivated. We also become frustrated and irritated with the One who told us to run the race, because we feel as if He is being insensitive to our plight. Often, our request of Him is to allow us to quit. However, how often do we come to the conclusion that quitting is not an option?

The real solution is to simply lay our bags down: anything that hinders our progress, particularly every form of sin.

This Is for You: Where are you going with those bags? If they are filled with things that are weighing you down, the answer is nowhere. When we run with weights, we sabotage our own success. In essence, we make our race virtually impossible to win. Step on the spiritual scale and see what is revealed. You just might find that it really is time for you to lose some weight.

God's Word to You: "Do you not know that those who run in a race all run, but one receives the prize? Run in such a way that you may obtain it" (1 Corinthians 9:24).

Day Twenty-Two Journal Discovery

1. What are the specific weights you are carrying? How are they impacting your race?

2. As you identify your weights, what is your strategy for laying them aside and not picking them back up?

3. How will losing your weights move you closer to living on purpose?

I Want My Space Back

*A wonderful realization will be the day you realize that you are
unique in all the world. There is nothing that is an accident. You
are a special combination for a purpose—and don't let them tell you
otherwise...only you can fulfill that tiny space that is yours.*

—Leo Buscaglia

NOT LONG AGO I was standing in my walk-in closet trying to figure
out what I was going to wear the next day. As I sorted through various
clothing items, trying to make my choice, I kept saying to myself, "I
really need more room in here. Why does it seem like I am running
out of space?"

Nevertheless, while I continued my sorting, I noticed something that
I had not given attention to before. As I looked at the various shelves
lined up against the wall, I noticed that three of them were filled with
nothing but bags. Over a period of time, I had saved a collection of
bags, in a variety of shapes and sizes, from previous shopping excursions.
I had paper bags, plastic bags, mesh bags, and cloth bags. I even had
bags tucked inside of other bags. The majority of the bags had been
shelved for a very long time. I looked around in awe of the fact that in
the excitement of bringing home my "new things" in those bags, I had

accumulated all these bags, and they were now consuming valuable space I needed to reclaim.

I further realized that many of the things that I had brought home in those bags were no longer new, and the excitement of having them had worn off. In fact, some of the things I had gotten were very old, some of the things were out of season, and some just didn't fit anymore. As a result of this natural experience, I was left with a powerful spiritual implication.

This Is for You: There have been times when we have allowed old bags to take up valuable space in our lives. These metaphorical bags could have once held "things" (something or someone) we were excited about and comfortable with bringing into our space. But now, for whatever reason, these "things" have gotten very old, are no longer a part of the season that God has us in, or no longer fit where we are, who we are, and where we are going.

Why are we keeping the bags? If we continue to hold on to bags from past experiences, we forfeit valuable space that God can use to fill our lives with His goodness. So, what are you going do with your bags? Are you content with leaving them in your life, or are you willing to get rid of the bags in an effort to let God know you have *space available*?

God's Word to You: "Therefore if anyone cleanses himself, he will be a vessel for honor, sanctified and useful for the Master, prepared for every good work" (2 Timothy 2:21).

Day Twenty-Three Journal Discovery

1. Who or what is occupying too much space in your life?

2. What do you need to do to reclaim your space?

3. How will these changes move you closer to living on purpose?

I Don't Feel So Good

God turns you from one feeling to another and teaches you by means of opposites, so that you will have two wings to fly—not one.

—Rumi

I HAVE A challenge for you. Set aside a day and pay attention to the number of times you hear someone say something about how he or she is feeling. Keep a record of what you hear in a journal. Add up your numbers at the end of the day.

Okay, I know many of you are saying to yourself right now, "I'm not doing that because I don't *feel* like it."

My point exactly.

I have come to realize just how much we are governed by our feelings. In this context, "feeling" is defined as, "An emotional state or disposition." While emotions are not a bad thing, being led solely by how we feel can be detrimental to our journey toward purposeful living.

Let me explain. In many of my life's experiences it has seemed as if everything was coming at me out of nowhere and all at once. During these times, as my grandma used to say, "I didn't know if I was coming or going." In the midst of it all, my focus turned completely towards my feelings. My decisions to do or not to do were solely based on my feelings. I also began to ponder negative thoughts such as, "I feel like

I'm not gonna make it." "I feel like the whole world is against me." "I feel like nobody understands." "I feel like giving up." As I allowed myself to be bombarded by these distressing emotions, I also began to speak those same things out of my mouth. As a result, what I was feeling began to consume every aspect of my life and ultimately created a personal downward spiral.

Moreover, because I had thought and spoken these things, I literally didn't physically feel so good. I didn't feel good in my mind, my will, or my emotions. I didn't feel like getting out of bed. I didn't feel like looking my best. I didn't feel like facing my situation and seeking God for resolution. My prayer was simple: "God, please help me not to feel so bad."

While drowning in these experiences, I began to realize that my only lifeline was to change my focus from what I was feeling to what I should be doing. I had to focus less on my desire to be comfortable and more on my need to be converted. I had to take my attention off my failures and center myself in faith for my future. I had to acknowledge the pain, but apply the peace. The real lesson was that if I was going to live my life on purpose, I had to be able to keep my feelings in proper perspective so that they would not interfere with what God desired to accomplish in my life.

This Is for You: What if our mothers had reneged on the idea of childbirth because the pain associated with labor and delivery would feel too bad? What if God didn't feel like providing us with the rich resources we have for our lives? Or, what if the journey to the cross had been based on feelings alone?

My point exactly!

God's Word to You: For we have not an high priest which cannot be touched with the feeling of our infirmities; but was in all points tempted like as we are, yet without sin (Hebrews 4:15, KJV).

Day Twenty-Four Journal Discovery

1. Assess your life at this very moment. How do your feelings impact what you see?

2. If you felt differently, would your life be different? Why or why not?

3. How will managing your feelings move you closer to living on purpose?

Independence Today

—⁓∰©

The God who gave us life gave us liberty at the same time.

—Thomas Jefferson

LAST NIGHT I had a very interesting discussion with a teenager. Our conversation began in a light-hearted manner, with general updates on life's happenings. However, after about two minutes, I could detect there was something going on beyond the superficial. As a result of some deeper questioning, the content of our dialogue changed from light-hearted to heart-felt. During that time, I observed that all things were not well in the soul (will, mind, and emotions) of this young person.

As our chat continued, he began to share a dilemma he was facing in a relationship. He explained how he had recently been bombarded with an accusatory line of questioning regarding his friends and whereabouts that left him feeling angry, confused, drained, and stuck. He stated he was angry because he was innocent, confused because he could not understand why it was happening, drained because it required so much of his energy trying to figure it out, and stuck because he had no idea where to go from here. He stated that no matter how hard he tried, the same thing in the relationship kept happening over and over again. After approximately ten minutes of his continuous venting and my attentive listening, he finally asked my advice. Needless to say, I was delighted beyond measure to give it to him.

I began my exchange with him with one word in the forefront of my thinking—"independence." *Webster's New World Dictionary* defines "independence" as "freedom from the influence or control of others." So speaking to him from this context, I began to share my assessment of the internal adjustments I believed he needed to make in order to free himself from the agony he was experiencing. At first, his continuous rebuttal was, "But what about her?" My response was simply, "What about her?" I informed him that he held sole responsibility for his choices regarding who or what influenced or controlled his actions. I reminded him that the Bible was very clear about "self-control" and said absolutely nothing about they-control, she-control, he-control, or it-control.

I suggested that while the issues of the other person could be problematic, those issues were not the problem—how he allowed those issues to impact him was the real problem and the true hindrance to his freedom. Too much time and energy is often expended on blaming others for the state in which we find ourselves. But, whose fault is it—really?

This Is for You: What are the dilemmas in your life that have left you feeling angry, confused, drained, and stuck? When challenged with this question, in many cases we relate our discomfort by focusing our attention on the issues of another person or situation. But how often have we asked ourselves, "What part am I playing in my own oppression?" I have learned that freedom is an internal choice that is not governed by outward circumstances. In order to continuously walk in that freedom, we must master living from the inside out, instead of the outside in. Remember, in any situation or circumstance, you are expected to control you. If you lose your control, you leave yourself vulnerable to the one who finds it. Choose independence today.

God's Word to You: "Stand fast therefore in the liberty by which Christ has made us free, and do not be entangled again with a yoke of bondage" (Galatians 5:1).

Day Twenty-Five Journal Discovery

1. Reflect on the definition of "independence." In what area(s) of your life have you lost your independence?

2. What part have you played in your loss?

3. What do you have to do to regain your independence and move closer to living on purpose?

What Lies Beneath?

Within you right now is the power to do things you never dreamed possible. This power becomes available to you just as soon as you can change your beliefs.

—Maxwell Maltz

ONE OF THE things I enjoy doing in my spare time is getting into my car on a nice evening, driving around various neighborhoods, and enjoying the beauty and character of the houses. I also enjoy looking into real estate guides and reading the descriptions of houses that are on the market for sale. Recently, as I perused one of the guides, I made a fascinating discovery. Along with the picture of each house, there was a statement regarding the type of foundation on which the house was built. As I read each description, I noticed that the foundations were described as being built either on a concrete slab or on a crawl space.

Not being familiar with the differences, I did some research. I began by looking at the meaning of a foundation. According to *The American Heritage Dictionary*, it is described as "The basis on which a thing stands, is founded, or is supported." My research also revealed that "Concrete is a hard building material made of sand and gravel, bonded together with cement." Therefore, it is extremely solid and rock-like. However, a crawl space is an unfinished space under the floor, which allows easy access to wiring and plumbing. The question is, to whom and to what are you allowing access to your plumbing and wiring? As a result of this investigation, I considered the spiritual connections.

For many of us, we have built our spiritual foundations on a crawl space. Because of this, we have allowed people and things to get into those unfinished spaces in our lives and gain easy access to our spiritual wiring and plumbing. Here is the problem—in the natural world, the purpose of wiring is to keep a connection to the power source. So spiritually speaking, if someone or something is tampering with our wiring, we are certain to feel a power shortage. We feel we have no power to change, no power to succeed, no power to overcome, no power to prosper, and no power to live victoriously. In actuality, our connection to the power source has been jeopardized.

Moreover, plumbing consists of pipes and fixtures for the distribution of water and the disposal of sewage. Now, if there is interference or tampering with our spiritual plumbing, the living waters of life that we should give out and should be characteristic of our walk in Christ cannot flow. Therefore, we become dried up faucets, unable to give to those who are thirsty. More importantly, if we are unable to adequately dispose of the proverbial sewage that sometimes comes or others bring into our lives, we will find ourselves spiritually impacted with a back-up of toxic waste that will ultimately lead to long-term spiritual damage or even our spiritual death.

This Is for You: What unfinished crawl space have you left available for easy access? Who or what have you allowed into that space? Where is the break in your connection with God, our Power Source? What are the areas in your life that have ceased to flow with rivers of living waters? In what areas are you experiencing a toxic back-up?

Our foundation, the basis on which we stand, must be the solid rock of Jesus Christ. Otherwise, we are standing on shaky ground. It is time for a foundation inspection to determine what really lies beneath.

God's Word to You: "He is like a man building a house who dug deep and laid the foundation on the rock. And when the flood arose, the stream beat vehemently against that house, and could not shake it, for it was founded on the rock" (Luke 6:48).

Day Twenty-Six Journal Discovery

1. How do you describe the foundation on which you currently stand in your life?

2. In what ways have you allowed access to your foundation? How has it impeded your progress?

3. What foundational changes will move you closer to living on purpose?

May I Take Your Order, Please?

Too often we underestimate the power of a touch, a smile, a kind word, a listening ear, an honest compliment, or the smallest act of caring, all of which have the potential to turn a life around.

—Leo Buscaglia

I AM CONSTANTLY fascinated by the customer service I receive when I go to fast-food establishments. More than anything, I find myself captivated by the energy it takes for any individual to be so discourteous. To date, I have had enough experiences to write a book entitled, *Adventures of the Drive-Through*. I have encountered the good, the bad, and too often, the ugly when placing a simple order. The exchange sounds like this:

"May I take your order?"

"Yes, I would like a number seven."

"What drink?"

"Sweet tea."

"Drive around and get your total at the window."

After my money is snatched out of my hand and my food is practically thrown at me, the window immediately closes in my face without a "thank you," "good-bye," or "have a nice day."

Customarily, I would leave these experiences with a change in my attitude and my own private mental outburst with thoughts like, "I don't know why you're mad at me." "I didn't tell you to get this job." "You act as if I'm the one making you work here." "I hope the next job you get makes you a little happier than this one."

Recently, after an encounter with a young lady at the drive through, I went through one of my self-righteous mind-storms. At its conclusion, deep down in my spirit came a question: "Instead of complaining about the service you are getting, how can you serve her?"

Instantaneously my thought was, "I am not obligated to serve someone who mistreats me." But the truth of the matter is, I was wrong. Not only am I obligated, but I can sabotage my own blessings by not doing so. To serve in God's sight means to act towards another in a specified way that brings Him glory. Serving that pleases God is not predicated on how we feel. In fact, we are compelled to "pray for those who spitefully use us and persecute us" (Matthew 5:44). Therefore, serving in spite of how we feel brings honor to Him and produces virtue in us.

I am by no means suggesting that this is an easy task. But I can remember the times in my life where my attitude was very bad, my disposition was volatile, and my demeanor was unpleasant. Why? Because I was hurting. I lashed out at others. I was defensive and offensive at the same time. This happened because hurting people hurt other people.

Nevertheless, one of the things that moved me out of this place was God sending special people into my life to serve me through their words, actions, and care. I didn't deserve it and did not always welcome it. But in hindsight, their godly acts towards me are what ultimately changed my downward spiral.

This Is for You: Many of you have people in your life that have mistreated you, persecuted you, and spitefully used you. Instead of retaliating and negatively responding, ask God to show you how to act toward them in a specific way that brings Him glory. The person you are serving may not change (that's sad). The person you are serving may turn completely around (that's awesome). However, the person God will cause you to become in the process (priceless).

God's Word to You: "For you, brethren, have been called to liberty; only do not use liberty as an opportunity for the flesh, but through love serve one another" (Galatians 5:13).

Day Twenty-Seven Journal Discovery

1. Who are the people in your life that are mistreating or wronging you in any way? What has been your response?

2. How can you change your response to that person or those people in a way that will bring glory to God?

3. How will wholeheartedly choosing to serve others move you closer to living on purpose?

I Can't Feel a Thing

You're a perfectly valuable, creative, worthwhile person simply because you exist. And no amount of triumphs or tribulations can ever change that. Unconditional self-acceptance is the core of a peaceful mind.

—St. Francis de Sales

SINCE I WAS a little girl, I have dreaded trips to the dentist. However, I recently had a dental appointment and was given enough anesthesia to paralyze a pony. (At least that's what it felt like.) From my nose down, there was no feeling in my face. Although I am very familiar with how to talk, through desensitized lips, my words just didn't seem to sound quite right. On top of all that, I was losing vanity points by the moment because I could not manage to keep the dribble from running down the side of my face, due to the loss of control of the mechanisms that are supposed keep my mouth closed.

Nevertheless, after leaving the dentist's office, the effects of the anesthetic became most apparent to me. As I walked out in public, I dropped my head or looked away from people because I was very conscious of my inability to smile without my face being distorted. I also avoided conversation because my words were slurred and unclear. When in the company of others, I kept my hand over my mouth in an attempt to disguise the fact that I had something going on. This was all a result of going through an experience that had left me *numb*.

Merriam-Webster defines "numb" as, "Deprived of the power to feel or move normally, total loss of sensation." Just like my experience at the dentist, many of us have gone through life experiences that have left us numb. As a result, we have lost our power to feel or function normally. In many instances we have lost our ability to smile. Or, if we do smile, it is often distorted by the hurt that has consumed our hearts. We have also avoided conversation because we can't find the words to adequately communicate what and how we feel. Because of this, we think we are better off just not talking, and we become emotionally unresponsive. When there are occasions in which we have to be in the company others, we hide or disguise the fact that there really is something going on.

I have come to understand in this case that the definition of "numb" really is "nobody understands my battle."

This Is for You: When we are in the midst of difficult and painful experiences, we can sometimes believe that it is impossible for anyone to relate to where we are. We feel we are in the battle alone. As a result, we shut down, desensitize, and become cold and indifferent. The danger in remaining in a state of numbness for too long is it can result in permanent damage. Ask yourself this question: "What do I need to do to get my feeling back?"

God's Word to You: "For we do not have a High Priest who cannot sympathize with our weaknesses" (Hebrews 4:15).

Day Twenty-Eight Journal Discovery

1. In what area(s) of your life are you experiencing numbness? Who or what helped you get there?

2. What would be different if you could regain your feeling?

3. What action are you prepared to take to move you out of your state of numbness? How will taking this action move you closer to living on purpose?

Who's Afraid of the Big Bad Wolf?

To him who is in fear everything rustles.

—Sophocles

WHEN I WAS a little girl, I loved listening to fairytales and nursery rhymes. One of my favorite stories was "The Three Little Pigs." Because it came in audio form, I could play the album on the stereo, read the accompanying book, look at the illustrations, and sing along with the music. I thought the pigs were adorable, and I loved the houses they built out of sticks, straw, and bricks. But I also remember the horror I felt every time the Big Bad Wolf entered the scene. At that time, the music would change from happy to daunting. The pictures would show the wolf creeping up on the houses in which the pigs felt secure. Because they were not alert, they didn't even know he was outside. Although I always knew how the story was going to end, I was still afraid every time the Big Bad Wolf threatened to huff and puff and blow their houses down.

Since that time, I have had many personal encounters where the "Big Bad Wolf" has shown up in my life at the door of my heart and mind, huffing, puffing, and trying to blow me down. Just like the pigs, when he appeared, I had a false sense of security and did not recognize he was present. But, I quickly became aware of his existence after feeling the hostile winds of adversity he blew into my life. As a result of the damage and devastation, I became apprehensive regarding making a move towards progress. I felt hesitant in my ability to make decisions regarding the direction for my life. I felt intimidated by others who appeared to have it all or were seemingly able to do it all. I felt discouraged by my self-perceived inability to find and pursue my purpose. I felt panic-stricken at the thought of living the rest of my days on earth in this pit. In essence, I felt the paralyzing impact of *fear*.

I recall an experience where fear's grip had consumed my life and left me in a debilitating stupor. I knew that I could not go backwards, but I was too afraid to move forward. I had been offered advice from others, whose advice ranged from I should "just get over it" to "move on with life." But the weakening blows of fear had beaten me into a catatonic state that kept me in extreme dysfunction.

However, in the midst of my quandary from this incapacitating experience, the Holy Spirit posed one question to me: "What would you do if you weren't afraid?" In other words, if you were not allowing fear to rule your life, what awesome things could you really accomplish for the purpose for which you were created?

This Is for You: What would you do if fear was not a factor? What goal would you reach? What next step would you take? What unfinished task would you complete? What career would you pursue? What healthy relationships would you attract? What unhealthy relationships would you let go? What doors of opportunities would you walk through? What doors of failure would you close? What final decisions would you make? What direction would you follow?

Fear keeps us from doing three things: 1) it keeps us from really knowing who we are; 2) it keeps us from walking in faith; and 3) it keeps us from using our gifts and pursuing our purpose. To conquer fear, we must use the power that is ours though the Holy Spirit, walk in the perfect love that causes us to put away fear, and invite the same sound mind to be in us that was also in Christ Jesus.

"Fear not" is mentioned 365 times in the Bible. Therefore, not one of your days should be spent consumed with fear. This is day one. How will you spend the remaining 364 days of your year?

God's Word to You: "For God hath not given us the spirit of fear; but of power, and of love, and of a sound mind" (2 Timothy 1:7).

Day Twenty-Nine Journal Discovery

1. In what areas of your life are you experiencing fear? How did you get there?

2. What do you believe could happen in your life if you were not afraid? What would you do? What would you allow God to do?

3. How will you confront your fear in a way that will move you closer to living on purpose?

Shake Well Before Using

*Therefore we do not lose heart. Even though our outward man is
perishing, yet the inward man is being renewed day by day.*
— 2 Corinthians 4:16

WHEN MY CHILDREN were younger and experienced childhood
illnesses that required an antibiotic, the medication always came in liquid
form, with instructions to take a certain dosage for a specific number
of times per day. Along with the explicit instructions was a general
directive to "shake well before using." According to Dr. Kate Kelly, "It
is important to ensure that the active ingredients in a suspension are
properly dispersed throughout the vehicle before administration."

"Shake well before use" is a common reminder given by pharmacists
to patients who receive oral suspensions. Yet, what happens if these
instructions are not followed? Dr. Kelly suggests that, "If a suspension
is unshaken or if it is inadequately shaken, it could lead to a significant
inconsistency in dosage."

Another spiritual implication occurs to me with this information.
Each of us is born with active ingredients. These are the gifts, talents,
and abilities that God planned for us before the foundation of the world
and deposited in us while we were still in our mothers' wombs. These
ingredients were given to us so that we could minister (be a medicine)

to those in need of what God has formulated within us. Nevertheless, if allowed to sit idle for an extended period of time in our lives, these active ingredients settle at the bottom of our souls. The problem is that in this state of inactivity, we lose our potency and become inconsistent in our quantity and quality to others. In other words, unless we are shaken, we are not equipped to maximize the benefits of what God created on the inside of us.

While we can cognitively understand this premise, the difficulty arises in our emotions. Let's face it, none of us looks forward to being shaken. Why? Because it does not feel good. It is often an agonizingly painful process. However, in God's infinite wisdom, shaking is not only allowed, but recommended. Think about the times in Scripture where those that God used mightily first went through a period of tumultuous shaking. These were not exercises in futility on God's part, but they were strategically planned and carefully orchestrated events that would ultimately lead those He used to eternally impact the lives of others.

God does the same in and for us. He loves us too much not to use situations and circumstances in our lives to shake up the active ingredients that are a necessary part of our purpose. Therefore, we do Him and ourselves a grave disservice when we allow our emotions (fear, dread, anxiety, and resentment) to get in the way of the process. Instead, we must understand that in order to impact the kingdom of God to the degree He has designed for our lives, He must shake us well before using.

This Is for You: As I reflect on many experiences in my life, I see my greatest growth and ministry to others has come as a result of times of shaking. In fact, during the times that I felt closest to God, and the most anointed for His service, there was a "whole lotta' shakin' goin' on" in my life. But the benefits have been an invaluable part of my journey. If I would not have had those episodes of shaking, everything that God had invested in me would still be lying dormant in my will, my mind, and my emotions. However, the shaking process moved me out of complacency, depression, doubt, and solitude, and it moved self-deprecating behaviors into a place of consistency in my dosage to others, for His glory. Therefore, I am most grateful that He loved me enough to shake me.

God's Word to You: "So may God shake out each man from his house, and from his property, who does not perform this promise. Even thus may he be shaken out and emptied" (Nehemiah 5:13).

Day Thirty Journal Discovery

1. As you take a realistic look at the concept of being shaken, what are your thoughts?

2. Understanding the benefits of being shaken, what are your thoughts?

3. How will being shaken move you closer to living on purpose?

Do the Math

—⁊⁊⃝

Friendships multiply joys and divide griefs.
—Henry George Bohn

OVER THE COURSE of my life, I have had many lessons that have taught me relationship principles. These lessons have come as a result of trial and error. Because we are not born knowing how to be in relationship with each other, life often presents us with opportunities to learn. These experiences can be filled with good, bad, and ugly experiences. In the words of Al Green, these pursuits can be filled with "Love and Happiness, or they can leave us feeling like Tina Turner: 'What's Love Got to Do with It?'" Nevertheless, if we are going to maintain a sense of health and well-being, we cannot avoid relationships. So then, the question becomes, "What kind of relationships do I desire to have in my life?"

I'm glad you asked that question.

When I consider the relationships that I have or have had in my lifetime, they all have had something in common—*math*. The relationships that failed, the ones that were seasonal, and the ones that were consistent were all based on the laws and principles of addition, subtraction, division, or multiplication.

For instance, the relationships that brought me the greatest joy, peace, and contentment have been the ones that have added to my life in one way or another. They have served to enhance my gifts, talents, and abilities, and served to help me consistently pursue my purpose. They have been authentically refreshing and have been a blessing from God that made me rich and not sorrowful.

On the other hand, I recall the relationships that brought me the most heartache and pain were those that seemingly took from me and gave me nothing in return. There was no mutuality in actions or deeds. I made deposits, but was never afforded the opportunity to make withdrawals. I was there when they needed me, but they did a disappearing act when I needed them. They subtracted from my identity, which in turn hindered the plans and purpose that God had for my life. They lowered my confidence, self-esteem, and ambition. These relationships had minus signs written all over them.

There were other relationships that had a wonderful beginning, but ended horribly. At the onset, it seemed that all the right ingredients were there for harmonious interaction. I felt comfortable and allowed my guard to be minimized because of what I perceived to be genuine care and concern. However, as the relationships progressed, I began to see behavior contrary to what was being stated verbally. There were extremely divisive tendencies and actions that multiplied minuscule issues to the point of overwhelmingly burdensome propagation.

Consider what this means. According the *American Heritage Dictionary*, "addition" is defined as, "a component that is added to something to improve it." "Subtraction" is defined as, "removing a part from the whole." "Division" is "the splitting of a group." And finally, "multiplication" is, "the process of becoming larger or more numerous."

My point—do your own math. If you find that there are relationships in your life that are improving you and building upon who and what God created you to be, while adding to your God-given purpose and destiny, then keep them. However, if you are in relationships that remove any part of the whole person God desires for you to be, or splits the things in your life that should stay together, or exacerbates issues, turning them into sheer drama, then it is time for you to employ your arithmetic skills and make some changes.

This Is for You: When you do the math in your life, what do you find? "Math is the science of dealing with the logic of quantity, profile, and arrangement." In order for us to have the relationships in our lives that are pleasing to God, we must use our judgment and discernment regarding quantity, profile, and arrangement of those who come into our lives. Now go ahead and prepare for your math test.

God's Word to You: "But seek first the kingdom of God and His righteousness, and all these things shall be added to you" (Matthew 6:33).

Day Thirty-One Journal Discover

1. What math problems have you gotten wrong in your past relationships? What present equations do you need to give attention to?

2. Are you prepared to make the necessary adjustment to ensure that your relationships are reflective of what is pleasing to God? If so, how will you proceed? If not, why?

3. How will the changes you make move you closer to living on purpose?

Conclusion

THROUGH INTENSE INTERNAL examinations and discoveries, God has brought me face-to-face with myself. He has opened hidden areas in my life and revealed unidentified, undeveloped places that are vital to fulfilling the plans He has for me. As a result of my many transformational encounters, I have reclaimed my voice, established my power, collected my confidence, pursued my purpose, salvaged my independence, and settled into my peace. In essence, I have found and taken my marble back.

In fact, this book is one of those marbles. It is a manifestation of my own journey through the good, the bad, the highs, the lows, the hills, and the valleys. But most of all, it is a representation of the work of God in my life. To a degree, this book is a recovery of many things lost and a testimony of what it really means to be found.

I am convinced that everything He has brought me through has been purpose-driven to bring me to a place in His Kingdom for such a time as this. I know that before the foundation of the world God had a plan in mind for my existence. I further believe that since the day I accepted Christ and committed to following Him, He has moved me closer and closer to my destiny. Therefore, in the midst of the difficult times, the painful times, the good times, and all the times in between, through the guidance of the Holy Spirit, I am confident that God orchestrated my past, positioned my present, and prepared me for my future.

Thus, the loss of my marble in 1969 was essentially a set-up for my success. In fact, my times in the fire, in the wilderness, and in the pit have increased my growth and faith to an extent I never would have imagined. For this reason, I am a woman changed and humbly grateful.

Now, let's all go show and tell about our marbles.

Let Us Pray ...

Father,

This really was for me. My journey of discovery has been life-changing. Thank you for divine revelation in so many areas of my life. I know now more than ever that I have been fearfully and wonderfully made and that you have glorious plans for my life. As I go forward, I do so with an assurance that I will fulfill the purpose for which I was created. I go forward with healing in my will, my mind, and my emotions. I go forward believing that the good work that You have begun in me, You will perform it until the day of Christ. Thank you.

In the name of Jesus,

Amen.

Today's Date_____

Works Consulted

Agricultural Utilization Institute. (2001). "Nutritional Labeling." Retrieved December 8, 2007, from http://www.auri.org.

Boultinghouse, P. 2000. *Hugs for Sisters*. West Monroe, LA: Howard Publishing Co., Inc.

Dooley, K. 2003. *Good Stuff*. Malvern, PA: Progressive Business Publications.

FaithPoint Press. 2005. *A Spoonful of Sugar for Women*. China: Cliff Road Books.

Federal Communications Commission. (2007). "Emergency Broadcast System." Retrieved December 13, 2007, from http://www.fcc.gov/eb/easfact.html.

Heald, C. 2005. *Becoming a Woman of Freedom*. Colorado Springs, CO: Navpress.

Howard. S. 2004. *Hugs for your Birthday*. West Monroe, LA: Howard Publishing Co., Inc.

Kelly, K. 2005. *Shake Well before Dispensing* [Electronic version]. Pharmacy Times, 18.

Merriam-Webster Online. (2007–2008). http://www.m-w.com.

Spirit Filled Life Bible. 1991. New King James Version. Nashville, TN: Thomas Nelson Publishers.

The American Heritage Dictionary of the English Language—fourth edition. 2003. Houghton Mifflin Company.

The American Heritage Science Dictionary of the English Language. 2002. Houghton Mifflin Company.

The Holy Bible. 1972. King James Version. Nashville, TN: Thomas Nelson Publishers.

The New International Webster's Pocket Quote Dictionary. 2002. Trident Press International.

Think Exists quotations. n.d. Retrieved multiple dates, December 2007–January 2008, from http://www.thinkexist.com.

Women of Faith. 2006. *Laughter & Latte: Joyful Inspiration for Women.* Nashville, TN: J. Countryman, a division of Thomas Nelson.

Pleasant Word

To order additional copies of this title call:
1-877-421-READ (7323)
or please visit our Web site at
www.pleasantwordbooks.com

If you enjoyed this quality custom-published book,
drop by our Web site for more books and information.

www.winepressgroup.com

"Your partner in custom publishing."

To contact the author:

Katrina E. Spigner
P.O. Box 4173
Columbia, South Carolina 29240
Web site Address: www.katrinaspigner.com

*Please include your testimony or help you received from this book
when you contact Katrina. Your prayer requests are welcome.*

LaVergne, TN USA
16 September 2009
158046LV00003B/4/P